TESTIMONIALS FROM EARLY READERS
AND TESTERS OF *CLOCKWORK*

"*Clockwork* had a radical impact on my personal approach to business. One of our companies acquired a record-breaking 22,000 customers in just five days, and our other one just had its three most profitable months in eight years of business, with no sign of slowing down. Oh, and both happened during an extended sabbatical largely made possible by internalizing and working toward the designing phase (the fourth and highest D)."

—RYAN LANGFORD,
CEO, Ultimate Bundles

"Implementing the *Clockwork* principles into our business this past year has been a total game-changer. As the visionary and chief content creator, I've been freer than ever before to do the things that only I can do, while I trust my team to take care of the rest. We've eliminated bottlenecks and learned how to use tracking and measuring to make much smarter decisions. Even better—my team is actually happier as a result!"

—RUTH SOUKUP,
author and CEO and
founder, Living Well Spending Less Inc.

"Since implementing the framework and principles taught in *Clockwork*, my business has released me. I am no longer being run by my business; rather I am running the business. Thanks to *Clockwork*, we are about to set off on a four-week trip as we travel across Canada work free for the summer—a dream come true to be able to fully step away from the business and the business still fully operational."

—ASHLEY BROWN,
owner and creative director,
She Implements and Nuvitzo Dance Studio

CLOCKWORK

ALSO BY MIKE MICHALOWICZ

The Toilet Paper Entrepreneur

The Pumpkin Plan

Surge

Profit First

MIKE MICHALOWICZ

CLOCKWORK

DESIGN YOUR BUSINESS TO RUN ITSELF

PORTFOLIO / PENGUIN

Portfolio/Penguin
An imprint of Penguin Random House LLC
375 Hudson Street
New York, New York 10014

Most Portfolio books are available at a discount when purchased in quantity for sales
promotions or corporate use. Special editions, which include personalized covers,
excerpts, and corporate imprints, can be created when purchased in large
quantities. For more information, please call (212) 572-2232 or e-mail
specialmarkets@penguinrandomhouse.com. Your local bookstore can also assist
with discounted bulk purchases using the Penguin Random House corporate
Business-to-Business program. For assistance in locating a participating retailer,
e-mail B2B@penguinrandomhouse.com.

Library of Congress Cataloging-in-Publication Data

Names: Michalowicz, Mike, author.
Title: Clockwork: design your business to run itself / Mike Michalowicz.
Description: New York City : Portfolio, 2018.
Identifiers: LCCN 2018015553 (print) | LCCN 2018021396 (ebook) | ISBN
9780525534020 (ebook) | ISBN 9780525534013 (hardback)
Subjects: LCSH: Small business. | Time management. | BISAC: BUSINESS &
ECONOMICS / Entrepreneurship. | BUSINESS & ECONOMICS / Small Business. |
BUSINESS & ECONOMICS / Time Management.
Classification: LCC HD2341 (ebook) | LCC HD2341 .M524 2018 (print) | DDC
658.02/2–dc23
LC record available at https://lccn.loc.gov/2018015553

Printed in the United States of America
1 3 5 7 9 10 8 6 4 2

Book design by Pauline Neuwirth

For Jake Michalowicz. Wuz up, my brah?

CONTENTS

CONTENTS

INTRODUCTION

"It's two a.m. and I am writing you out of desperation."

That is the opening line from an email I received from Celeste,* an entrepreneur who reached out to me for help. Over the last eight years, I've received countless emails from readers and from people who have heard my message about eradicating entrepreneurial poverty in my books, my speeches, an article, or on a video or podcast. I respond to all of them and save quite a few, and this is the one that lit a fire under me to finish this book.

The email continued: "I own a preschool. We make no money. I haven't taken a salary since we started. I'm racking up debt. And tonight, I am broken. Not just financially, but in my soul. I am convinced an immediate termination of my life would be the fastest resolution to my predicament."

Reading that email, I felt as if my heart dropped to my stom-

---

* Name changed.

ach. I was concerned—no, terrified—for Celeste's life. At the same time, I recognized her vulnerability.

"Please understand, I am not sending you a suicide note," Celeste went on, "and I am not at risk for such stupidity at the moment. That decision would just leave the burden to my family. But if I was single, I would be gone. You see, I have double pneumonia right now. I can't afford someone to clean our preschool, and for the last four hours, I have been scrubbing the floors and cleaning the walls. I am exhausted. I am crying, and stop only because I am too exhausted to cry. I am starving for sleep. I am so ill, yet I can't sleep because my worry keeps me up. The only thing I have left to give my business is my time and that is now depleted, too."

My heart broke for Celeste. I'd been in a similar state of mind a few times in my life as an entrepreneur, and I knew countless others who had been lower than low, desperate for a solution. The last lines of the email will stay with me forever:

"What has become of my dream? I am trapped. I am exhausted. I can't work more than I already do. Or maybe I can. Maybe my work is the slow suicide I am thinking of."

What has become of my dream? Does that question ring true for you? It did for me when I read the email. We work, and work, and work, and work, and before we know it, the business idea we once proudly shared with our friends, the plan we outlined on a whiteboard, the vision we shared with our first employees, all seems like a dim memory of an unobtainable goal.

Normally, I would ask permission to share an email from a reader, but I'm not sure how to reach Celeste, and I'm hoping that maybe she will read this and get in touch. I responded to her email multiple times, but I never heard back, and I didn't have any luck tracking her down. I still think of her today, and share her story as a cautionary tale.

Celeste, if you're reading this, please email me again. I will help you. If you'd rather not contact me, then please know this: It's not you that is holding your business back. It's surely your systems—and those systems can be fixed.

Perhaps you can relate to Celeste; perhaps (I hope) you're in a less dire situation, managing to keep up the grind week after week and keep the wheels of your business turning. Whatever the case, chances are you don't ever feel like you can ease up, or spend *less* time and effort on your business. Why is that?

Most entrepreneurs I know do everything. Even when we bring on help, we spend just as much time, if not more, telling the staff *how* to do all the things that we are supposed to no longer worry about. We put out fires. We stay up late. We put out more fires. We work weekends and holidays, flake on commitments to family, and bail on nights out with friends. We put out even more fires. We push on, we push harder, we don't get enough sleep.

But here's the irony: Even when things are going well with our business, we are still exhausted. We have to work even harder when things are good, because "who knows how long this will last?" And the growth opportunities we know we should grab by the horns, the visionary work that is crucial to explosive growth, the stuff we *love* to do, is set aside day after day until that notepad with all of our ideas is lost under a sea of papers and to-do lists, never to be found again.

We're blowing it. We're all blowing it.

"Work harder" is the mantra of both the growing and the collapsing business. Work harder is the mantra of every entrepreneur, every business owner, every A-player employee, and every person just struggling to keep up. Our perverted pride about working longer, faster, and harder than everyone else in our industry has taken over. Instead of running one marathon, we are trying to sprint ten. Unless something changes, those of us who buy into this way of life are headed for a breakdown. And maybe double pneumonia to boot.

Maybe you can relate. If you can, I want you to know you are not the only one who is going through this. You are not the only entrepreneur who feels they must work harder, who is exhausted and wondering how long they can sustain this level of work. You're not the only business owner who wonders why all your improvements haven't improved your bottom line, or garnered you more clients, or helped you retain employees, or simply given you back just a little bit of your precious time. You're not the only person who is reading this book because you feel stuck, and you're desperate for answers . . . and a nap. According to an article on 20SomethingFinance.com, the United States is the "most overworked developed nation in the world" (G. E. Miller, January 2, 2018). And here's the irony: Americans are 400 percent more productive than we were in 1950. And yet, as employees, we work more hours and get less time off than employees in most countries. As entrepreneurs and business owners, our workload is even greater. As for time off? We don't take any.

I started writing this book when I asked myself a key question: Could my business achieve the size, profitability, and impact I envisioned without me doing all (or any) of the work? This question triggered my half-decade quest for answers—for me, and for the business owners and entrepreneurs I serve. *For you.*

If you're unfamiliar with my previous books, or if you've yet to hear me speak, I want you to know that my mission in life is to *eradicate entrepreneurial poverty.* I am committed to never again letting an entrepreneur live with lack: Lack of money. Lack of time. Lack of life. In my book *Profit First,* I sought to defeat one of the monsters that drives most entrepreneurs to despair: the lack of money. In this book, I'm going to help you slay an even bigger monster: the lack of time.

Whatever answers you are looking for, in this book you'll find real, actionable business efficiency strategies that have worked for countless entrepreneurs, numerous business owners, and for me, too.

The goal is not to find more hours in your day. That is the brute force approach to business operations, and even when you pull it off, you'll just fill that time with more work, anyway. The goal is organizational efficiency. In this book you'll learn how to make simple but powerful shifts in your mind-set and day-to-day operations that will make your business run on automatic. I'm talking predictable outcomes, my overworked friend. I'm talking real, sustained growth. I'm talking a thriving workplace culture. I'm talking freedom to focus on what you do best, and what you *love* to do. And that, compadre, is the only way to build a truly successful business—by freeing ourselves to do the work we do best and the work we love most.

We are also going to free you from the grind. We are going to relieve you from the constant pull on your time, your body, your mind . . . *and* your bank account. Yes, it is possible to feel at ease about your business. Yes, it is possible to regain the optimism you felt when you first started your company. Yes, it is possible to scale your business without killing yourself or sacrificing your own happiness.

You need to stop doing everything. You need to streamline your business so it can run itself. I'm talking about your business running like a well-oiled machine, run by a highly efficient team that is aligned with your objectives and values. A business that runs, well, like clockwork.

The process you will discover in this book is ridiculously simple. You will not find shortcuts, tricks, or hacks to packing more in. Instead, you will discover how to get the work done that matters most, avoid the stuff that doesn't, and have the wisdom to know the difference. (Yeah, I borrowed a little bit from the Serenity Prayer. Serenity may seem like an impossible goal for most overworked visionaries like you. Heck, you'd probably settle for sanity at this point. But by following the seven steps I outline in this book, serenity is definitely back on the table, baby!)

Life is about impact, not hours. On my deathbed, I will be asking myself if I fulfilled my life's purpose, if I grew as an individual, if I truly served you and others, and if I deeply and actively loved my family and friends. If I may be so bold, I think you will be asking the same.

It's time to join the elite Clockwork Club. Seriously, make your stance and join us, first at our website, Clockwork.life,* and then at the beach one day soon. It's time to get back to what you love— in your life, in your work, and in your business. It's time to implement strategies with ease and joy. It's time to bring balance back to your life. This book will help you do all of that.

That is my wholehearted promise to you.

---

* To make it super easy for you to get all the free resources for this book, I created a site called Clockwork.life. Everything you need for this book, including a Clockwork Quick Start Guide, is there. Additionally, if you want professional help from a noncorporate consultant, a get-your-hands-dirty expert, I have a small business that does just that at RunLikeClockwork.com. Note that Clockwork.life is not a .com, but a .life, because the Clockwork Club is a lifestyle. And RunLikeClockwork.com is a .com, because it is all about our company serving your company.

CHAPTER ONE

WHY YOUR BUSINESS IS (STILL) STUCK

As is traditional for many people born and bred in the Garden State, every summer my wife and I pack up the kids and meet my sister and her family for a week of fun at the Jersey shore. Up until a few years ago, our summer trip went something like this: Everyone would spend the day at the beach and then the adults would start happy hour around four p.m., talk a big game about hanging out until the sun rises, and then promptly fall asleep by seven p.m.

Except I hardly ever made it to happy hour or spent much time at the beach. I was working. Always. When I wasn't focused on completing a project, or in a meeting, I was trying to sneak "a few minutes" to check emails. When I did make it outside to join everyone, I was so distracted by thoughts of work that I wasn't really there. This caused me stress and annoyed the heck out of my family.

Every year, I tried to break the "workcation" habit. I had the same plan: I would get all of my work done in advance so that "*this* time," I could finally enjoy my vacation and be fully present with my family. Then, I thought, I would return from vacation with no work to do, or at least very little, and easily get back up to speed. But my plan never worked out. Often, it was just the opposite of what I planned.

The last time I tried to prove that I really could work this vacation plan was a total disaster. A problem with a client came up the afternoon of the day before we were to leave. I can't even remember what the problem was, but, at the time, I thought it was important enough to work on the solution well into the night. Then I stayed up even later to finish the work I had to do before the client crisis.

It was nearly dawn before I made it back home from work. I slept for three hours, then headed to Long Beach Island. (If you aren't from New Jersey, I want you to know that LBI is the real Jersey shore, *not* the boozefest of a show that lays claim to it.) Before I went to the beach, I decided to check my email to "make sure everything was okay." It wasn't. The rest of my day was spent making calls and sending emails. Even when I made it to the beach the next day, my mind was on the business and my body was dying for sleep. Yet again, I wasn't really there. My family's vacation was compromised, too, because my tension spread like smoke in a bar. One person can really stink up the place and ruin everyone else's fun.

My wife was frustrated with my workaholic ways, and so, one afternoon, she sent me for a walk on the beach—without my phone. As I looked at the beachfront houses, I thought, "The people who vacation at those mega-mansions have it all figured out." They had financial freedom. They could take vacations and not worry about work. They could enjoy themselves and come back to a business ticking along, still growing, still making money. That's what I wanted.

But as I looked closer, I saw person after person sitting on their decks frantically plugging away on their laptops. I even saw people on the beach, with laptops perched precariously on their knees, scared of sand getting in the keyboard while they tried to shield their screens from the glare of the sun. The people I assumed had it all together weren't any different from me. They were all working on vacation. *What the f?*

At this point in my life, I had built and sold one multimillion-dollar business to private equity and another one to a Fortune 500 company, written two business books, and spent a good part of my year speaking to thousands of entrepreneurs about how to grow their companies quickly and organically. Sounds like I was living the dream, right? You would think that I had retired my workaholic badge for good. But stressing out about work on yet another vacation proved I hadn't. I wasn't even close. And it was clear: I was definitely not alone. Neither are you.

THE SOLUTION IS NOT THE SOLUTION

I thought the cure for my workaholicism was better productivity. If I could just do more, faster, I could find more time for my family, for my health, for fun, and to *get back to doing the work I really loved.* The work that fed my soul.

I was wrong.

In an effort to be more productive, I tried it all: Focus apps, the Pomodoro method, working in blocks. Starting my day at four a.m. Ending my day at four a.m. Lists on yellow notepads. Lists on my phone. Lists of just five things. Lists of everything. Back to lists on yellow notepads. The "Don't Break the Chain" method, which quickly led me to the "Chain Myself to My Desk" method. No matter what hack or technique I tried, no matter how productive I became, I still slipped into bed at night long after I should have, and woke up the next morning way earlier than I should have, with a to-do list that seemed to have magically grown overnight. Maybe I did things faster, but I surely didn't work fewer hours. If anything, I worked more. Maybe I was making progress on many small projects, but many more new projects were filling up my plate. And my time was still not my own. All my years of studying productivity had given me nothing but more work. It was an epic fail.

If you haven't tried some of the productivity strategies I rattled off like bad failed diet plans, I'm sure you have your *own* list. An entire industry is built around the desire to do more, faster. Podcasts, articles, and books; mastermind groups and coaches; productivity challenges, calendars, journals, and software. We buy into the next productivity solution someone recommends because we're desperate. Desperate to grow our companies by getting more done faster, and managing all our work without losing our minds.

Some productivity experts are getting out of the "time hacks" game. As I was doing the research for this book, I befriended former productivity maven Chris Winfield. He had just completed one of his fabled retreats where he teaches twenty or so business leaders and professionals how to do more things in less time.

We met for coffee in New York City near Lincoln Center so he could teach me what it really took to be productive. I was ready to finally discover the productivity secret that would release me from my stress-ridden life. I arrived forty-five minutes early. I couldn't wait to find the ultimate hack. Chris arrived exactly on time, to the minute—typical of a productivity expert.

After we made the obligatory "this coffee is really good" comments, Chris looked me right in the eye and said, "Productivity is shit."

"Wha . . . ?!" I said, nearly spitting out my deliciously balanced Fazenda Santa Ines coffee. I can become a bit of a coffee snob (or, my preferred title, a "beanologist") when I have forty-five minutes to kill before a meeting.

"It's shit, bro. I have been teaching productivity for years and everyone I have taught is actually working more, including me."

I said, "I don't get it. Why is that?"

"Because productivity leaves everything on your plate. Productivity allows you to do more, faster. The pivotal word being 'you.' *You* can do more, therefore *you* in fact do more, and *you* do it all. Even when you say you are outsourcing the work, you really aren't, because you can't outsource the decisions. You are giving one task to someone else, but they come back at you with one million questions. You actually need to work even more, when you try to not do the work."

Chris continued. "I'm telling you, Mike. Productivity is hurting a lot of people. I'm done dying from it, and I'm done preaching about it, too. I am leaving the industry so that I can start working less, begin making more, and live life."

Mind. Blown.

It turns out that productivity doesn't get you out of the doing; it just gets you doing more. I had started my clockwork quest by seeking the wrong holy grail!

REVISITING PARKINSON'S LAW

You and I both know extremely productive people who work sixteen hours a day. You and I absolutely know the "I do best when I cram" people. Maybe it's you. Once upon a time, it surely was me.

It took me about fifteen years to figure this one out. I actually wore the productivity master's badge of honor—the workaholic badge. I was a proud member. I was the fastest task-ticker-offer in the land. (What? It's a thing.)

In my book *Profit First*, I applied Parkinson's Law—"our consumption of a resource expands to meet its supply"—to profit. Just as we use all the time we have allocated for a project to finish it, we also spend the money we have, which is why most entrepreneurs rarely earn as much as their employees, much less turn a profit. The more money we have to spend, the more we spend. The more time we have, the more of it we spend working. You get the idea.

The fix to this behavior is ridonkulously simple: limit the resource and you limit your utilization of it. For example, when, after you collect revenue, you allocate profit first and hide it away (in a remote bank account), you have less money to spend. So guess what? You spend less. When you don't readily have access to all the cash flowing through your business, you are forced to find ways to run your business with less.

And now that we're talking about time, Parkinson's Law is even more relevant. Whatever time you give yourself to work, you will use. Nights, weekends, vacations—if you think you need it, you'll work right through your time off. This is the root cause of the failure of productivity. The goal of productivity is to get as much done as quickly as possible. The problem is, because you've prioritized a seemingly endless amount of time to running your business, you'll continuously find a way to fill up the time. The more productive you are, the more you can take on. The more you take on, the more productive you have to be. Do you see how productivity is a trap?

If you're like me and most entrepreneurs I meet, you use the time you saved to do more work—just as Chris said. And not the work that feeds your soul. Not the work that could truly make a difference for your business. No, you do the next urgent thing.

You put out the fires, and then you do the next tasks that will be the next fires, until you're interrupted by some other even more urgent thing that pops up. You keep working your ass off and feeling as though the more progress you make, the more work you have.

It was only after I met Chris Winfield that it dawned on me: Yes, productivity is important; we all need to make the best use of our time. To be unproductive is like sinning against the business gods. (Plus, sittin' around eating Cheetos and watching Thigh-Master infomercials all day isn't going to move anyone's business forward.) But in time, I came to understand the real holy grail is organizational efficiency. Productivity gets you in the ballpark. Organizational efficiency gets you hitting home runs.

Organizational efficiency is when all the gears of your business mesh together in harmony. It is the ultimate in leverage, because you design your company's resources to work in concert, maximizing their output. Organizational efficiency is where you are accessing the best talents of your team (even a team of one) to do the most important work. It is about managing resources so that the important work gets done, instead of always rushing to do what's most urgent. It is not about working harder. It is all about working smarter.

For far too many of us, twenty years of business ownership is celebrated by realizing that we survived twenty years of a continuous near-death experience. But it doesn't have to be that way. You are not alone. There are millions of people just like you. I was one of them, and I'm here with you. In fact, I'm still progressing further and further on this stuff, even as I write this. I still have to remind myself to work smarter, not harder; it's so easy to fall back into believing there's a magic productivity hack that will save the day. Whatever choices you made to get you to this day, it's okay. It got you here. You're in the park. Now, put down that frankfurter and sauerkraut, and step on the field, crackerjack. You are about to hit the entrepreneurial homer of a lifetime. You can take a selfie right now, pointing to the stars, because you and your business are about to launch. Take your time and make a great pose. I'll wait.

So what's the fix? We change the system around us so that we don't need to change (we really can't change much anyway) and set up the system so that it will channel our natural tendencies to achieve the outcomes we want.

Part of the Clockwork solution is to actually restrict time, to use Parkinson's Law to our advantage. But that alone won't get us off the hamster wheel. When we give ourselves less time, we also need to figure out *where* to focus the remaining time. It's not about doing more with less. It's about doing less with less to achieve more. You need to do the right tasks with *your* restricted time and have other people do the right tasks with *their* restricted time.

In other words, a business that runs like clockwork is about selective efficiency, not mass productivity.

PLAYING IT SAFE

My first business coach, Frank Minutolo,* saw me through three startups and two acquisitions, including one sale to a Fortune 500. Frank brought the Japanese company Konica to the United States, and grew it from a startup to $100 million. After he exited, he pursued his life's calling: coaching a handpicked group of young(ish) entrepreneurs. I was one of the lucky thirty or so who could call him their adviser.

---

* I still see Frank on occasion, even though he is long retired now. The man can't resist a lunch on me, and I can't resist learning from him.

I'll forever be indebted to Frank for his no-nonsense, sage advice. I based my book *The Pumpkin Plan* on the simple strategy to rapid organic growth that he taught me. It started with our first face-to-face meeting. He had spent four hours with our team evaluating every aspect of our businesses, and then we had a one-on-one immediately after.

Frank looks a little like Regis Philbin and sounds a little like the Godfather. "Mike," he told me, "you need to get smarter about growing your business. You don't want to put in all this effort, endure all this stress, only to end up with nothing to show for it. Your retirement will be spent in a rusty lawn chair with one nut hanging out of your shorts, while you regret your life of toil." One nut? What the hell? That description was the weirdest thing I'd ever heard. It is just something that once you picture it, it can't be unseen.

It turns out that vividly descriptive visions of your client in a decrepit state, peppered with some flagrant genitalia references, is a shockingly effective sales strategy. I hired Frank that day, and he subsequently ensured that I avoided that nasty future by helping me rapidly grow and sell two companies. But it was only after ten years of working together that I finally got what he was trying to tell me. Fear can be a massive catalyst for change.

One afternoon, I took Frank out to lunch at Fuddruckers and finally asked him why he would share such a bizarre story on the very first day I met him. Frank chuckled one of those old-guy chuckles where laughter turns into a minor fit of choking.

"The point of that story," Frank explained, "is that the roadblock is you. The problem is the draw of the familiar. Entrepreneurs aren't that different from any other human, in that when something is familiar, it becomes comfortable. Entrepreneurs—you included, Mike—work like animals. And while you say you 'hate it' or 'won't do it anymore,' the truth is, you are familiar with it. And when you are familiar with something, as ugly as it is, it is easiest to keep doing it. Doing what's familiar will land you in that rusty lawn chair, with a nut hanging out of your shorts.

"My goal is to make you more fearful of doing what's safe and familiar, than taking the leap to the promising new. I wanted you to be terrified of the path you were on. I used your fear of where you were comfortably headed to move you to the new uncomfortable place you needed to go."

As painful as it can be to be stuck in the grind, our belief that we need to "work more" and "work harder" becomes familiar. Despite our exhaustion, the situation is comfortable, so the same problems yield the same solutions. Working long hours does not require us to step out of our comfort zone, or learn something new, or let go of our ego-driven need to micromanage.

Entrepreneurs have become way too comfortable with the hardship, so they keep doing the things that keep them in that state. If you want to make your business the most efficient it can be, you must stop doing what you are doing, which is getting in your own way. You doing the work, or inserting yourself in other people's work, may be all you know to this point. It may be very comfortable by now. Stop doing it.

THE SURVIVAL TRAP

If you've read my previous books, you have probably heard about the Survival Trap. I have talked about the Survival Trap for a long time now. And, still, I'm going to return to the Survival Trap because, unfortunately, this is the state most of us entrepreneurs end up in, and very few of us ever escape from.

The Survival Trap is what I call that never-ending cycle of reacting to whatever comes up in your business—be it a problem or an opportunity—in order to move on. It's a trap because as we respond to what is urgent rather than what is important, we get the satisfaction of fixing a problem. The adrenaline rush of saving something—the account, the order, the pitch, the entire damn day—makes us feel as though we are making progress in our business, but really, we are stuck in a reactionary cycle. We jump all about, fixing this, saving that. As a result, our business careens to the right, then to the left. Then we throw it in reverse, and jam it forward. Our business is a web of misdirection, and over the years it becomes a knotted mess—all because we were just trying to survive.

The Survival Trap is all about getting through today at the utter disregard for tomorrow. It's about doing what is familiar, as Frank warned. We feel good that we survived the day. But then, at some distant point in the future, we wake up and realize that years and years of work didn't move us forward one iota, that merely trying to survive is a trap that results in a long, drawn-out drowning of our business and our willpower.

Sadly, you will discover that living in the Survival Trap leads to a very trashy day-to-day life of quick highs, deep lows, and doing anything to make a buck. Quite frankly, it is not the life of the coveted entrepreneur; it is the life, shrouded in shame, of the entreprewhore. I too was one. I was addicted to doing whatever anyone wanted at whatever price they offered. I prostituted my business to survive just one more day, and then I continued that behavior as I expanded into multiple disastrous businesses.

Ten years ago, I cleaned up my act, and got out for good. I started by taking my profit first, as I shared in *Profit First*. Then, by focusing on my Top Clients, my business grew fast and organically. Today, I am in the final stages of reclaiming my life because I have designed my business to run on automatic. You are about to do the same.

In *Profit First* I wrote a little section that was the seed of this book: "Sustained profitability depends on efficiency. You can't become efficient in crisis. In crisis, we justify making money at any cost, right now, even if it means skipping taxes or selling our souls. In crises, the Survival Trap becomes our modus operandi—until our survival strategies create a new, more devastating crisis that scares us straight or, more commonly, scares us right out of business."

Was Celeste, the preschool owner I mentioned in the introduction, caught in the Survival Trap? Most definitely. She was experiencing the extreme version of the trap. You may be comfortable in your trap. Maybe it's manageable. Maybe you take pride in managing it. But what does that matter if you're still in the trap?

The Survival Trap is what's keeping you from driving toward your vision, or meeting short- or long-term goals. In some sense, we know this. We feel guilty about that five-year plan we haven't looked at in seven years. We see other businesses launching new initiatives or products in alignment with trends, and we wonder how they found the time to predict and respond to the changes in our industry. (They must have superpowers, right?) We know we're behind in terms of making the best use of innovations in technology and workplace culture. And we know that in order to take our business to the next level, we need to get back to our visionary roots—the ideas and plans and *heart* we had when we first started our business.

It's hard to escape the Survival Trap because your business constantly pulls you back into keeping it afloat. But I'm going to show you how to escape it for good by designing your business to run itself and freeing yourself to do only what you want, when you want. So let's get busy getting *unbusy*, why don't we?

THE SEVEN STEPS OF CLOCKWORK

In the next seven chapters, we'll cover the steps you'll need to take to make your business run like clockwork. One step may take longer than another, and you may find yourself having to go back and improve one of the steps from time to time. This process may take you two days or two months, but if you follow the steps, you'll get there.

For a business to grow and serve its client base, it needs to get things done. This is the Doing part of a business. The business must also orchestrate its efforts so that all the people and systems are moving the business forward in a complementary fashion. This is the Design of a business. As people on your team work together, their communications will consist of making Decisions and Delegating work that must be accomplished. How you allocate your business's time between the Doing, Deciding, Delegating, and Designing functions is called your 4D Mix, and getting it in the right proportions is crucial to helping your business run itself.

Most micro-enterprises and small businesses spend too much time Doing. Imagine that solopreneur who is running around like a chicken without a head doing everything, or that small business where everyone—including the boss—is working crazy hours with no time allocated for planning. The goal of clock-working your business is to move you toward Designing it to run itself while other people or resources take care of the Doing part. To make this happen, we need to start with you and get clarity about how much time you spend Doing, and to do *that* we need to analyze your 4D Mix and that of your company.

As is true with any problem or opportunity in life, if you want to improve things, you need to know your baseline. Once we know that, we take deliberate and direct steps to get your company (and you) where you want it to be. The optimal 4D Mix is when the business spends 80 percent of its time Doing, 2 percent of the time making Decisions for others, 8 percent of the time Delegating outcomes, and 10 percent of the time being Designed for greater efficiency, better results, and less cost in the process. Regardless of whether you have one employee, one thousand, or somewhere in between, the optimal 4D Mix stays the same.

Here are the seven steps to make your business run itself:

1. **Analyze the 4D Mix—Set the benchmark levels for the blend of Doing, Deciding, Delegating, and Designing at which your business is currently operating.** A clockwork business balances getting work done, managing resources, and constant improvement. In the first phase of making your company run itself, we will do a simple time analysis to see how much is being spent in each of the four categories. And once we know, then you can adjust your company to the optimal 4D Mix.

2. **Declare the Corporate Queen Bee Role—Identify the core function in your business that is the biggest determinant of your company's success.** Within every company there exists a single function that is the most significant determinant of the company's health. It is where the uniqueness of your offering meets the best talents of you and/or your staff. It is what you declare the company's success will hinge on. I call it the Queen Bee Role, or QBR. When this function is at full throttle, the business thrives, and when it is slowed or stopped, the entire business suffers. Every business has a QBR. You must identify and declare your company's QBR, and as you improve its performance your entire business's performance will elevate.

The QBR is the "thrive factor" for your business, and you must decide what you want it to be.

3. **Protect and Serve the Queen Bee Role—Empower your team to ensure the biggest determinant of your company's success is guarded and fulfilled.** The QBR is such a critical role to your business that every employee, even if they are not the ones serving the QBR, needs to know what it is and how to protect and serve it. In a highly efficient business, the QBR is always the priority and systems are in place so that the people and resources who serve it are not taken away from it. Only when the QBR is humming along, can all people in the business do their own most important work (this is called their Primary Job).

4. **Capture Systems—Document or record the systems you already have in place so your team can do the work the way you want them to.** Even though it may not seem that you have systems, you do. In fact, every business at every stage has all the systems it needs. Those systems simply need to be captured, trashed, transferred, and/or trimmed. Every entrepreneur and employee has a way of executing various tasks, but often they are undocumented and non-transferable. Using a simple evaluation and capture method you will impart that information to your team or freelancers with ease. Hint: You will *not* be creating a manual. Both the creation and consumption of manuals is inefficient and therefore has no room in a clockwork business.

5. **Balance the Team—Adjust roles and shift resources to maximize the efficiency and quality of the company's offering.** Businesses are like organisms; they grow and contract and change. To perform optimally you must match the inherent strength traits of employees to the jobs that

need them most. Instead of a traditional top-down organization chart, an optimized company is more like a web. You never restrict employees to one job function. Instead, an efficient organization identifies the natural-strength traits of the employee and matches them to the tasks that benefit the most from those traits.

6. **Make the Commitment—Devote your process to serve a specific consumer need in a specific way.** The biggest cause of business inefficiency is variability. The more services you provide to a wider mix of customers, the more variability you have, and the harder it becomes to provide extraordinary and consistent services. In this step, you will identify the best type of customer to serve, and determine the fewest products/services that will serve them at the highest level.

7. **Become a Clockwork Business—Free the business from dependency on you, and free yourself from dependency on the business.** A clockwork business is a business that delivers consistent results, including growth goals, without your active involvement. As you are less available for the business, it will naturally become designed to run without you. In this step, you will learn how to create a business "dashboard" that enables you to stay on top of your business, even if you're not there.

That's it. Seven steps. In that order. You will discover and execute these seven steps throughout the rest of the book. As you go through this process, you will feel frustrated, or stuck, and want to give up. Don't freak out; those are just signs that you are getting comfortable with the uncomfortable new stuff I am teaching you. Again, don't freak out, and don't you dare ever stop. And as a result, you will experience a business that runs on automatic, just like clockwork.

WHY YOUR BUSINESS IS (STILL) STUCK

SEVEN STAGES OF CLOCKWORK

STAGE	CORE CONCEPT	KEY ACTION
1	**THE 4D MIX** The four types of work are Doing, Deciding, Delegating, and Designing	Conduct a time analysis and categorize the type of work
2	**THE QBR** The core function you decide to hinge your company's success on	Declare your company's QBR and identify who is serving it
3	**PROTECT AND SERVE THE QBR** The core function of your business is always the priority	Educate your team on the QBR and empower them to guard and/or fulfill the QBR
4	**CAPTURE SYSTEMS** You already have all the systems created for your business	Use the trash, transfer, or trim method to free time for Design work, QBR work, and Primary Job work
5	**BALANCE THE TEAM** An optimized organization chart is a web-like structure	Match the strongest traits of team members to the tasks that most need those traits
6	**THE COMMITMENT** Your business strength comes first, then you target the customer who will benefit most from it	Identify, focus, and cater to the consumers who will most benefit from your unique offering
7	**BUSINESS ON AUTOMATIC** Doing makes you work for the business, Designing makes the business work for you	Take the four-week vacation

FIGURE 1

Time is everything. Every. Single. Thing. Time is the only thing in the universe (until someone invents a time machine) that is not renewable. Either you use it wisely, or you don't. Time will still tick, tick, tick away no matter how you spend it. I suspect even right now, you may have made a few nervous looks at the clock, as time races by, hoping you can cram in this book (and your work) faster. Am I right? Even just a little bit? If you are experiencing that, I want you to know it's not your fault; it's Parkinson's Law. And I want you to know you are actually in a good position. Better said, you are in a salvageable position. Your business likely has demand and you are delivering on it (although not efficiently). What we are going to do is make a few simple tweaks to make your business run like a well-oiled machine and, in the process, give you back that ever-precious time that seems to move, more slowly and comfortably.

I want to be clear that this book is *not* about doing more with the time you have. It's about your business doing more with the time *it* has, and about giving you freedom to do other things with your time. It's about getting your life back while you grow the business of your dreams. That can happen. Actually, it *does* happen, all the time, for other businesses. Our job, today, is to do it for yours. But for this to work, you need to be all in on this with me. Are you ready? Good. Let's get to work.

Scratch that. Let's get to *less* work.

 ## CLOCKWORK IN ACTION

Your primary focus is to design the flow of work through your company so that other people and other things can get the work done. Commit to putting your company's output first and your productivity second. How do you do this? Simple . . . you will find better answers when you ask better questions. Stop asking "*How* do I get more done?" and start asking, "*What* are the most important things to get done?" and "*Who* will get this work done?"

At the end of each following chapter, I'll share action steps you can accomplish quickly—usually in thirty minutes or less—and still experience big progress. For this first chapter, I only have one action step for you, but it is perhaps the most important. It will force an immediate adjustment in how you view your role in moving your business forward. The step? I want you to commit . . . to me.

Send me an email at Mike@OperationVacation.me with a subject line that reads: "My Clockwork Commitment." That way, I can easily spot it among the other emails I get. Then, in the body of the email, please write something like:

"Starting today, I commit to designing my business to run itself." Include any other information you think is relevant, such as why you won't stand for the old way of running your business anymore or what this means to you and your family.

Why email me? Because, if you're like me, when you commit to someone else, your follow-through skyrockets. Remember, I personally respond to all emails from readers (albeit super slowly at times). I look forward to receiving yours.

P.S. Make note of that unique domain for my email, OperationVacation.me. I know it might not make sense at the moment, but it is me who gets it. And soon enough, very soon in fact, you will learn what Operation Vacation is all about.

CHAPTER TWO

STEP ONE: ANALYZE YOUR COMPANY'S TIME

The first time Scott and Elise Grice visited me in my New Jersey office, we talked about laundry for a solid twenty minutes. Yes, you read that right. Laundry. Specifically, how they do three weeks' worth of laundry—for both of them—in an hour and ten minutes . . . while running errands. I've never given more than a passing thought to laundry, and yet, as Scott and Elise explained how they streamlined it, I was riveted. Seriously, they are systems *ninjas*.

As our conversation progressed, I learned why systems are so important to Scott and Elise. Founders of Hey, Sweet Pea, a branding team originally based in Austin, Texas, the couple has taught and developed brands for more than 1,400 creative entrepreneurs (think photographers, writers, stylists, graphic designers). Two years into their business, they were handling thirty to forty custom branding clients at a time. To give you a sense of how successful they were, other companies in their industry typically handled four to five custom branding clients at a time. They were rocking it—until life intervened.

In 2013, Elise contracted West Nile virus, which landed her in the hospital, and it quickly escalated to bacterial meningitis. Over the next two months, she spent six weeks in the hospital and two more completely immobilized at home or in an ambulance going back to the hospital. Because of her illness, every time Elise so much as looked at a screen—her phone, her tablet, her laptop— she experienced shooting pains in her head. Too exhausted to even type on a keyboard, Elise couldn't work at all. She had to call it quits, and that meant she and Scott would also have to quit their business, because when Elise "The Coach" Grice couldn't work, the business team couldn't run any "plays."

"We had a team of nine contractors producing work, but Elise was the creative director, and we couldn't send anything to the clients until she approved it," Scott explained. "Since she couldn't look at a screen to approve work, everything backed up. The business came to a grinding halt and we couldn't invoice anyone."

Two months after she contracted the disease, Scott and Elise found themselves sitting on her hospital bed, surrounded by medical bills, wondering what they would do if she never got better. "We were both crying. I said to Elise, 'If you don't fully recover, we can't run this business. You are the only one who has the ability to approve this stuff, no one else, including me, can.' We were making payroll out of our savings account. I was terrified for my wife and I was terrified for our business. I had no idea what we were going to do."

Their business was entirely dependent on Elise, and in just two months without her, the wildly successful company was in wildly dire straits. It took only *two months*. This is what we business owners fear the most—that if we step away from our businesses, if we check out, even for a few days, our businesses will suffer or die. I know I've felt this countless times, and used this fear as a justifiable reason to work, work, work, and then work some more. I suspect you have, too. (Here's a little secret: The work is never done.)

We'll return to the Grices and find out whether their business survived in a few pages, but if you fear what will happen to your businesses if you take a break—or are forced to take a break—it's a big sign, as in flashing-neon-billboard big, that your business needs to be designed to run itself. If you had systems in place to keep your business running with or without you, you wouldn't worry about taking time off. I think you know that, because you're reading this book. What you may not realize is that getting your business to run without you begins *with* you, and how you view your role in your company. We first must move you from Doing to Designing.

As I said in the previous chapter, productivity is a trap because, ultimately, the work is still being done by you. Most of us are used to doing whatever it takes to keep our businesses afloat—and the operative word here is "doing." In the early days, we have no choice but to take on every role in our hopeful startups. There is even that cheesy phraseology that circulates with us entrepreneurs, "I'm the CEO, the CBW, and everything in between." I'm sure you have heard that one. You know, the chief executive officer, the chief bottle washer, and everything in between. Cute. But not a way to grow an efficient business.

Entrepreneurs are natural DIYers—HGTV has nothing on us. Shoot, we should have our own channel! We do everything as we build an early stage business, because we *must* do everything. We can't afford to hire others, and we still have the time to do everything. We aren't usually that good at most of it (even though we convince ourselves we are), but we get the stuff done well enough. While it makes sense that we have to take on many different roles when we first get our business off the ground, keeping it up is not healthy and not sustainable. Finally, we make that first hire, and even with the added financial pressure,* we feel some relief since we couldn't keep up the insane pace of doing everything. But the sprint-like pace in fact does not go away. Even when we hire people to help us—employees or subcontractors—we often still end up "doing" a ton of work—scratch that, *more* work—because we, like Elise in her branding business, are the linchpins.

Designing a business that runs itself is doable. In fact, it is very doable. To pull it off, you have to shift away from *Doing* and focus more and more of your time on *Designing* the flow of your business.

THE FOUR DS OF RUNNING A CLOCKWORK BUSINESS

There are four phases of activity that you engage in as an entrepreneur. These are "the four Ds"—Doing, Deciding, Delegating, and Designing. Although you are engaged in all four of these phases to varying degrees during the course of your business's evolution (you spent some time Designing your business before you launched it), and while your business will always have a mix of all four Ds, our goal is to get you, the entrepreneur, Doing less and Designing more.

Shifting from Doing to Designing is not a "Monday morning makeover" kind of shift. It's not a switch you flip; it's a throttle.

---

* The financial dilemma of hiring people is very difficult for small business owners. When you hire an employee, you might have to cut your own compensation, which is already sparse. So we delay hiring until we can afford the employee, but never get there. We are stuck between a rock and a hard place. Work even harder, which you can't. Or hire someone, whom you can't afford. There is a solution, though, which I explain in *Profit First*. I made a video explaining exactly how to address this situation successfully. It is available on the Clockwork.life page.

You build toward this. You become more and more of a designer over time, and there is no finish line.

1. **Doing:** This is the phase when you do everything yourself. You know it well and you do it well (enough). When you're a solopreneur, doing everything yourself is a necessity. This is where almost every startup starts, and where most of them get stuck, permanently. Of the twenty-eight million small businesses in the United States, more than twenty-two million don't have a single employee.* In other words, the owner is doing everything.

2. **Deciding:** In this phase, you assign tasks to other people. Whether they are full- or part-time employees, or freelancers, or contractors, they are really only task rabbits. They try to do the one task you gave them and then come back to you to ask questions, get your approval, have you solve problems, and help them come up with ideas. If there is any unexpected anomaly to the task at hand, the person comes back to you for your decision. When they finish a task, they either sit idle or ask you, "What should I do now?"

   Most entrepreneurs confuse Deciding with Delegating. If you assign a task to someone else but need to answer questions to get the task done, you are not Delegating—you are Deciding. Business owners who have two or three employees can get stuck spending most of their time in this phase. Your employees do the work, but because you make every decision for them, you're never able to grow beyond two or three employees. Work becomes a constant and distracting stream of

---

* www.forbes.com/sites/jasonnazar/2013/09/09/16-surprising-statistics-about -small-businesses/

questions from employees. It eventually gets so bad that you throw your hands up in frustration and make the decision to "go back to how it was before" and do all the work yourself. You get rid of your help, go solo for a while (because it is easier to just do work than to decide for everyone else), only to soon enough get overwhelmed with the work and then hire again, and return to getting frustrated with the Deciding phase. You flip-flop back and forth for the life of the business between doing the work and deciding for the few employees, over and over again.

3. **Delegating:** In this phase, you're able to assign the task to an employee as well as empower them to make decisions about executing that task. The person is fully accountable for the completion of the task. They are on their own. As you spend more of your time in the Delegating phase, you will start to feel some relief from your workload, but only if you delegate in the right way. Initially, you *must* reward your employees' ownership of a task— *not* the outcome—because the goal is to shift the responsibility for decision making from you to them. If they are punished for wrong decisions, you will only be training them to come back to you for decisions. You, too, have made wrong decisions in the past; that's how you grew. They will make wrong decisions, and that is how they will grow. The Delegating phase can be extremely difficult for entrepreneurs, because we can do everything perfectly (in our mind) and get frustrated when they don't. You must get past this perfection mind-set if you ever want your business to successfully run itself.

4. **Designing:** This is when you work on the ever-evolving vision for your company and the flow of the business to

support that vision. The business runs the day-to-day on its own. Shoot, you could even take a four-week vacation without the business missing a beat. (Put a pin in that.) When you are in this mode, you will not only be free from the daily grind, but you will also experience the most joy in your work. Your job is elevated to managing the business by numbers and fixing the flow of business when things aren't the way they are supposed to be. This is when you are no longer needed to do the work; you are now overseeing the work (to the degree you want to) and doing only the work you want to. This is the good life, my brothers and sisters.

DOING IS GETTING YOU NOWHERE

I can read your mind. I know, it's a little creepy. But you are my kindred spirit BFF, and I am sure I know what you're thinking right now: "I can't stop doing the work. I'm the only person who really knows how to do the X, Y, and Z around here. My staff is great and all, but they can only do their stuff. When it comes to the stuff I do, no one else can even come close. I am that committed. I am that good. I am the only one who will ever be able to do what I do. And when the sheeyat hits the fan, it's all me, baby. All me!"

Am I close? I think I am. It's not hard to read your mind, because I suspect you and I are not that different. It took me years to stop believing my own hype, and, truthfully, I still struggle with the urge to "just do everything myself." In my more than twenty years as an entrepreneur, "doing everything" was something I expected of myself. I was a "serious" entrepreneur. I did "whatever it took" to grow my business. And because I succeeded, I attributed much of that success to my "tireless" work ethic. Even when I had a staff of nearly thirty employees, I still burned the midnight oil, doing much of the work and overseeing the rest of it because "no one can ever do the stuff only I can do." I just wished that my employees would "step up" and "act like an owner." But they didn't. They just bothered me with an endless stream of questions. Notice all of the quotation marks in this paragraph? That's because most of my perceptions were, like I said, hype—total BS.

Again, as a business leader, your time is best spent *Designing* the work, not *Doing* the work. What do I mean by "Designing the work"? Let's use a football analogy. (Go Hokies!) It's the story of the team owner, the coach, and the players. The players are empowered to make split-second decisions in the field of play, the coach creates the game plan and calls the plays, and the team owner designs the team. The owner lays out the vision for the franchise, picks the coach(es) to manage the team, and then watches from afar as the team puts the game plan into action. For the outsider, it may be a bit confusing. It just looks like a rich old guy eating mini-wieners in the glassed-in suite. But there is much more going on than you can see. The owner is always optimizing every element of the franchise: the team, the sponsor deals, the seat sales and the up-sells, the marketing, the budget, etc.

As a designer, you think several steps ahead. You are strategic. You measure opportunities and risk. Is every move you make the right one? Of course not. But you measure the outcomes of your moves and make adjustments accordingly on your subsequent moves. And to be your company's designer you must get off the field and up in the suite. Just avoid those mini-wieners. Nothing good ever comes from those things.

Every entrepreneur starts out as a doer, because doing things is what we're good at. The problem arises when you get stuck in that phase, and all the Doing keeps you from your bigger vision of building a business. You're already familiar with Design work. It's what you loved when you first started—creating a vision for your company and considering the big, bold strategic moves you could make. So this is also the work that you have the firsthand knowledge to do effectively—direct the flow of the business. When you are spending most of your work time in Design mode, your company achieves absolute efficiency and scalability potential. As designer, you are giving your company your best—your genius, the genius that started it all. You are also removed from the day-to-day operations so that your business can run without you, which means it can also *grow* without you. Your purpose is to design the flow of your business, point it in the direction of growth, and then make strategic decisions to fix, change, and/or improve things when the flow is not right.

Even when we appreciate the value of Design work, most of us still devote too many hours to Doing. This doesn't just apply to the solopreneur who hasn't delegated anything yet, but also for leaders of teams of five, or fifty, or five hundred. Owners, managers, and C-suite teams can get trapped in the Doing just as much as any solopreneur.

A 2009 study by the Max Planck Institute for Biological Cybernetics in Tübingen, Germany, confirmed that people trying to find their way through a forest or a desert devoid of landmarks (and without the sun as a beacon) tend to walk in circles. People walked in circles as tight as sixty-six feet while thinking they were walking perfectly straight. That is like putting a blindfold on and trying to walk across a football field, the short way, one sideline to the other, and never making it across.

Researchers concluded that in the absence of clear markers of distance and direction, we make a continuous stream of micro adjustments to what we think is straight, but those adjustments are biased to one side more than the other. Our constantly changing sense of what is straight keeps us walking in a loop. We circle and circle, ultimately perishing, when we could have easily gotten out of the weeds by just walking straight.

You can overcome this tendency if you have a distinct landmark to move toward, and if you are lucky enough to be equipped with a compass or GPS. The distinct and distant landmark allows us to constantly recalibrate our direction and stay straight. Even when an obstacle presents itself, we can avoid it, move around it, or run from it, and then again spot our landmark and use it to correct our course.

Why am I telling you this? Because a business that doesn't devote time to determine where it wants to go, seek ways to get there, and identify the landmarks that will offer the most direct route is destined to spin in circles for eternity. The struggle to escape the Survival Trap is constant. The business owner and team toil away, month after month, year after year, hoping to move forward, but in the absence of a clear sense of direction, they are surprised and frustrated when they keep circling back to the same spot.

By becoming a designer of your business, your role is to define what your company is marching toward, identify the landmarks that signify progress, equip yourself and your team with the tools (for example, a dashboard that acts likes a business's GPS), and establish strategies to make the path safer, easier, faster, and more efficient (like building a bridge across a river).

A business can only experience extraordinary progress with extraordinary design. And you can only do that if you devote time to this most important endeavor. Time to establish what your company's Big Beautiful Audacious Noble Goal is. Time to think about the impact you are intending to have on your clients. Time to figure out the right strategy to achieve that impact. And time to determine what metrics you will use to measure the progress of your company and your team. This is your company's destination and your vision for it.

The worst part about walking in circles? We don't believe we are doing it even when we see proof. In the study by the German research group, participants were dropped in the middle of a German forest and another group in the Sahara Desert. With GPS tracking devices attached to them, they were given simple instructions: walk straight for a few hours. When the sun or moon was visible, people stayed on a somewhat direct course. But on a cloudy day or a night with no moonlight, people reverted to their looping pattern immediately. Worse yet, the terrain caused even more complications with direction, creating a channeling effect. People can't walk straight without a landmark, and when complications present themselves, they often put people in a whole new direction yet again.

Trying to build a business by just Doing and without Designing is like walking through a dense forest while blindfolded. It is inevitable you will walk in circles and be thrown into another course if you come across a substantial obstacle. Navigating the terrain of growing an organization needs a designer who looks beyond the constant stream of challenges and opportunities immediately in front of them and instead charts a path to success. And that designer is you. Yes, even if you've lost touch with the vision you once had, even if you feel you haven't seen your creativity in the last decade, and even if you wonder if you truly have what it takes to navigate your ship to new, prosperous shores—you are the best person for the "design" job. You can do it.

THE DELEGATION COMPLICATION

When you first want to scale your business, the Deciding phase comes quickly. The process is easy—hire people and tell them what to do. Getting them to do the work without your input? Not so easy. And we bring this problem on ourselves. Every time my staff had a question and came back to me for a decision, it made sense. They were new employees and they needed to learn the right way to do things—my way. So I gave them the answers they needed and sent them on their way to do the work. Plus, every time they had a question that only I could answer, it pumped my ego and fulfilled my need to feel important. I'm just being real with you here. And you need to be real with yourself, too: knowing what others don't is an ego boost.

I thought the need to answer everyone's questions would be short lived. They were learning the tools of the trade, and I expected the questions to slow down. But, oddly enough, they increased. The problem that I didn't realize, until it was too late, was that I was teaching them to always get the answers from me. All they ever mastered was the BuTSOOM system that I taught them. You know, the Bug the Shit Out of Me system.

I bet you have taught your team the BuTSOOM system, too. And I will bet you are all too familiar with how it goes down. It starts with the "better than sliced bread" moment. You bring on virtual help, or a part- or full-timer. On the first day, the only person more excited and anxious than that employee is you. Within days you're thinking, "This new hire, she is taking so much work off my hands. Why didn't I do this sooner? She is 'better than sliced bread.'"

The newbie has tons of questions, but that is to be expected. In fact, that is what you want: a learner. But a few weeks later, this person still has tons of questions. She's asking questions she should know the answer to by now. What is going on? Then, in a few more weeks or months, that new "bread" is now a total distraction. The questions never stop. You are pulled from your own work constantly to serve her. That is when you realize this bread is that lamely made, gluten-free kind. You know, it is about as flexible as concrete and has the rich flavor of cardboard. That is when you start to think, "It's just easier to do all the work myself."

When you give your employees all the answers, you block their learning. I suspect that when you first learned to drive a car, you only figured it out, for real, by driving the car. Yeah, you went through that six-hour, in-classroom driver's-ed course where you were told the gas pedal is on the right and the brake is on the left. But even with those instructions, when it actually came to driving the car, chances are you overaccelerated or hit the brake too hard. I bet that as you learned to steer a car, you went a little too tight and crushed a cone or two.

The learning—the true learning—is in the doing. You must experience it for it to become ingrained in you. Our employees must experience the decision making for it to become ingrained in *them*. The irony, of course, is when you hire someone to do the work, you specifically are doing it so you can reduce your work. But if you allow yourself to make all the decisions for them, your work increases, and their growth stops in its tracks.

Having to oversee my staff didn't reduce my hours. I actually worked more, because I was constantly pulled away from the work I should have been doing to make a decision for someone else. Then, when I got back to my work, I would have to sync up again, which as you know all too well, takes time. The distraction of being the decider made *me* super inefficient. Employees would put their work on hold as they waited their turn to ask me a question. They literally *stopped* taking action until I gave them direction. My work stopped and so did theirs! Trying to do my job and supervise my staff was like trying to type a letter *and* handwrite instructions at the same time. Try it. You can't do it.[*]

This experience led me to believe I had to get more work off my plate, so I would hire another person. And another. And another. Until I was making decisions for an entire team and trying to do my work at night, on weekends, at the crack o' dawn. As a result, the company became more inefficient, because all of those people were waiting for me to make decisions. Instead of capturing and utilizing the most powerful resource I had—their brains—we were all dependent on mine. As an added bonus, all those salaries drained my bank accounts.

I decided to get back to what worked—me and me alone. I fired everyone to get back to getting *my* stuff done. I thought that would be easier. I had romanticized notions of being the lone wolf entrepreneur who "Gets Shit Done." I was delusional; it was as if I forgot what it was like to do every job. The cycle started all over again. Flipping between Doing and Deciding is more common than you think. That's why most businesses don't ever get past one or two employees.

Answering their questions made my work wait, and doing my work made my employees wait for my answers. According to Daniel S. Vacanti, author of *Actionable Agile Metrics for Predictability: An Introduction*, more than 85 percent of a project's life span is spent in queue, waiting for something or someone. While waiting time is inefficient, it's also exhausting. If we can reduce waiting time, we can improve growth—and gain sanity.

Many businesses with fewer than three employees get stuck playing the waiting game, and in the back-and-forth between the doing and deciding phases. Business owners start with "I need to

---

[*] If you want to try to prove me wrong, please send me a video of you typing and writing at the same time. I would love to see it.

do it all" and move to "I need to hire people to do it." Then, when they discover their workload hasn't lightened up, and they are more stressed and strapped for cash than ever, they end up thinking, "Everyone is a moron, and I will fire them all and just do it myself," which eventually leads them back to "Oh, God, I can't keep doing this, I need to hire people desperately," and back around to "Is everyone on this planet an idiot?"

No, your people are not idiots. Far from it. They just need *you* to stop Doing and Deciding and start Delegating not just the deeds, but the decisions. For real.

I was chatting with Scott Oldford, founder of INFINITUS Marketing & Technology, when he said, "The biggest problem is that no one has taught entrepreneurs the mind-set of delegating. It's not that they don't know they need to delegate. They just need to get into the mind-set of letting go. Then, when they are committed to it, they need to do it the right way."

Scott explained that the delegating is a process. "First, you assign a task. Then you assign the responsibility. Then you ask them to own the results. Finally, you ask them to own the outcome, which is repeated results over time."

What could you accomplish if your staff was not focused on completing tasks, but on delivering outcomes for your company? That's a game-changer, right? We'll cover this in more detail in chapter four, but for now, let me just get your buy-in on the delegating concept. Ask yourself: Would my life be easier if my employees were empowered to make decisions, and I felt confident that they would routinely make decisions that would sustain and grow my business? Would my life be easier if my employees acted like owners?

It's a no-brainer, right? The only answer is, "Damn straight, Mike! My life would be an endless string of awesomeness, bee-yotch!"

When *your* desired outcome is also *their* desired outcome, you are better able to let go and let your team *do their jobs*. And it will be okay. It will be more than okay. You're going to be a delegating machine. You'll be the Oprah Winfrey of delegators: "You get a project! And you get a project! And *you* get a project!"

If you're going to save your Saturdays and your soul and scale your business, being acutely aware of what phase of the four Ds you are in is essential. Will you ever stop Doing entirely? Maybe not—but you will do a fraction of the work you do now, and you will transition to doing only the work you love.

Think for a moment about Jeff Bezos, the mastermind behind Amazon. On Thursday, July 27, 2017, the news broke that Jeff Bezos had unseated Bill Gates as the wealthiest person in the world. It was a momentary topping, as the stock market played back in favor of Bill Gates by the end of the day and Gates once again was the richest person on the planet.* Pick either entrepreneur. Gates and Bezos have both focused their energies on the Design phase from the get-go. But even today they do a little bit of the doing. You can bet your bottom dollar, when a major partnership is negotiated, Bill Gates participates in the deal. And when Amazon rolls out another game-changing product, not only does the design team test the prototypes, Bezos does a little test run himself. The Doing phase will never disappear fully for an entrepreneur; it will simply take up the least amount of time.

Deciding every little thing—you can kick that phase to the curb. You won't stop Deciding entirely; you will just move from making minor decisions to making only the most critical decisions as the people to whom you delegate become more comfortable making

---

* Within days of the announcement of Jeff Bezos momentarily being the world's richest man, with a cumulative wealth of more than $90 billion, Bill Browder, the CEO of Hermitage Capital Management, announced that Russian president Vladimir Putin was in fact the world's richest man, with estimated assets in excess of $200 billion. Gates and Bezos are duking it out at the $90 billion mark, and then this Russian monster of money walks into the ring and knocks everyone out. It sounds like *Rocky IV* to me. However, in this book I will not be using Putin as an example of how to run a business.

decisions on their own. As for Delegating, because your business will evolve and change, you'll have to dedicate some time for Delegating. You will delegate until you hire a delegator, whose Primary Job is to continually empower the team to make on-the-field decisions and protect you while you do the Design work. Reminder: This is not a switch from one phase to another; it is a throttle. The goal is for you to spend *most* of your work time controlling the flow of work and designing your company's future. If you want your business to run like clockwork, as Gates and Bezos have done, you must concentrate the majority of your effort into being a designer.

THE 4DS—TARGET PERCENTAGES

If you want to improve your body or your business or anything for that matter, you need to know what you intend to accomplish *and* where you are today. Setting a goal of losing one hundred pounds is not a good idea if you only weigh one fifty. Clarity comes from knowing your ideal target *and* where you are starting. That is what we are going to do for your business in this step.

FOUR TYPES OF WORK

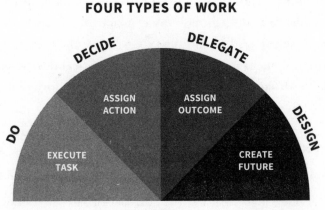

FIGURE 2

There are four ways in which people who work for a business serve that business. Every person in an organization is either Doing the work, Deciding for others about the work, Delegating the work to others, or Designing the work. As mentioned earlier, collectively I call this the 4Ds.

The 4Ds are being executed within your business and every other organization on this planet. This is true if your business is a company of one, one hundred thousand, or any number in between. And this is true for every single person at your company. From an intern to an executive board member, from the nice folks in C-suite to the sweet folks with feet on the street, everyone is working the 4Ds.

Each person in your organization is doing their own blend of the 4Ds, although you may not (yet) be deliberately directing it. Some people may be Doing work constantly. Another person may be Deciding what other people should be doing while Doing the work of ten people, and with the few seconds left trying to Design a forward-looking strategy. Sound familiar?

Collectively, the 4D work of each person combines to form a 4D Mix for your business. If the business is just you, the solopreneur, your own 4D Mix *is* the company's 4D Mix. If the company is multiple employees, the aggregation of each employee's 4Ds is the *company's* 4D Mix.

The ideal mix for a company is 80 percent (Doing), 2 percent (Deciding), 8 percent (Delegating), and 10 percent (Designing). (See figure 3 on page 38.) Why does a business need to dedicate so much time for Doing? Because businesses need to do things that customers want, and that creates value in the marketplace; that's how businesses make profit. The other 20 percent of that ideal company mix is spread over managing and guiding the business. For you to design your company to run itself, you need to master the mix. Simply put, you need to know what your company's 4D Mix is as compared to the optimal 4D Mix, and then use the Clockwork system to continually optimize your business.

Critically Important and Helpful Shortcut: Analyzing for the optimal ratio can be arduous and time consuming. Since business is dynamic, it is very difficult (perhaps impossible) to constantly nail down that ratio. So the one thing you should focus on, above all else, is the big piece, and that is the 80 percent of Doing time. Is your company spending most of its time serving clients (that is the 80 percent Doing), but not all of it? If you are at 95 percent Doing, you can tell instantly that there is not enough Designing or other work going on because there is only 5 percent of company time left for the other three Ds. If the Doing is at 60 percent, that also tells you that you're in trouble, since your business isn't spending enough time getting things done. So if you simply track the Doing and target 80 percent, the other three Ds will often come into alignment. Focus on spending as much of the remaining 20 percent on Designing, and the Delegating and Deciding will often just fall into place, as long as you

OPTIMAL 4D MIX

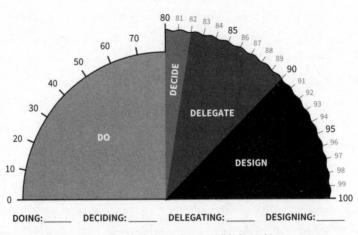

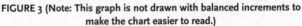

FIGURE 3 (Note: This graph is not drawn with balanced increments to make the chart easier to read.)

commit to empowering your employees to take ownership of their work.

Now that you know what the optimal mix is, let's figure out where your business is right now. We ultimately need to evaluate how all the people in your organization are utilizing their time, but since you are the one reading this book and quite possibly serving the QBR (more on that later), we need to analyze your mix first. And if you are a one-person business, then *you* are the business. No matter how many employees you have, it is important you understand this process and what it reveals about *your own* 4D Mix. This process will help you understand how to evaluate your company's 4D Mix.

Review the last five days you worked. If you maintain a calendar or task tracker, this may be relatively easy to do. To the best of your ability, write down each task you did and action you took for the five days we are evaluating.

1. On a piece of paper create six columns, titled Date, Activity, Start, Finish, Total Time, and Work Type (I also created a chart you can download at Clockwork.life). This is your Time Analysis Worksheet.

TIME ANALYSIS WORKSHEET

DATE	ACTIVITY	START	FINISH	TOTAL TIME	WORK TYPE
					DO | DECIDE | DELEGATE | DESIGN
					DO | DECIDE | DELEGATE | DESIGN
					DO | DECIDE | DELEGATE | DESIGN
					DO | DECIDE | DELEGATE | DESIGN
					DO | DECIDE | DELEGATE | DESIGN
					DO | DECIDE | DELEGATE | DESIGN
TOTAL TIME	DOING: _____	DECIDING: _____	DELEGATING: _____	DESIGNING: _____	

FIGURE 4

2. Fill out the form by writing down each work task or action you took during each of the five days. To make the process as easy as possible, do your best to recall one complete day at a time, and then repeat this for each of the five days.

3. In the Date column, write the day of the activity.

4. In the Activity column, write a few words that describe the task or action you took.

5. In the Start and Finish columns, write the times you started and finished the task. (This is only necessary when you do an Active Time Analysis. Since you are doing this one from recollection, skip the Start and Finish columns, and simply fill in the Total Time you spent on the task.)

6. As the final step, categorize the task as a Doing, Deciding, Delegating, or Designing activity. Or if you are using the form you downloaded from Clockwork.life, simply circle the appropriate activity category.

7. If you don't have good calendar records and are struggling to remember your last five days of work (welcome to the life of an entrepreneur), just complete the Time Analysis Worksheet as you go through the next five days. As you dig deeper into the Clockwork system yourself, and roll it out to your employees and colleagues, an Active Time Analysis is the most accurate approach. In this process, you will track the actions you take as you take them, ensuring you don't miss a thing.

THE ACTIVE ANALYSIS

Hang on—I'm about to throw a bunch of numbers at you. Like Dorothy in *The Wizard of Oz*, you may not want to walk through the woods to get to the Emerald City. For her, it was scary. For you, it may seem tedious or overwhelming. Percentages, percentages, percentages, oh my! I realize you might not be a business geek like me, who gets turned on by allocation exercises and analysis. But stick it out for me, would ya? You need this information to get where you're going. (Which, incidentally, I hope is the great land of Oz, not the dust bowl of Depression-era Kansas. Why *did* Dorothy want to go back, anyway?)

1. Get a fresh Time Analysis Worksheet as described in step 1 above.

2. As you go through the day, write down the date and the activity you are working on, along with the time you started it. Then get to work on that activity. The moment you shift to different work, any work—including a distracting question from a colleague, answering an urgent email, or heading out to lunch—quickly jot down the finish time for the current task (even if it is not finished . . . it is just finished for the moment). Then write down the new activity (e.g., answering your colleague's question) and when you start it. Then, once that activity is complete, fill out the time you finish it. Then do the same for the next task. Repeat for the entire day.

3. When the day's work is done, make sure all the date fields are completed. A line from top to bottom is adequate and effective (this is a book on efficiency, after all). Then look at each task for the day and mark the type of work it is on the sheet: Doing, Deciding, Delegating, or Designing. Only choose one for each task. If you are unsure, choose the lowest of the levels you are considering (Doing being lowest and Designing being highest). I know this is laborious, but it is only five days of your life,

it is very revealing (you may be surprised by the gap between your perception and reality), and it is a critical step in getting your business to run on automatic. You need clarity on where you are right here, right now, so that we can quickly move you to where you need to be.

4. Once the Time Analysis Worksheet is completed for all five days, add up the total time you spent Doing. Then add up the total time for Deciding. Then Delegating. And, finally, do it for Designing. Put the totals on the bottom of the form, and keep the form for future analysis.

5. With the totals for each of the 4Ds, create a gauge graphic (or fill out the one I created for you below or download one at Clockwork.life) that shows your 4D Mix. Calculate the percentages by dividing the total of each D into the sum of all 4Ds. For example, if you spent forty-five hours Doing, fourteen hours Deciding, one hour Delegating, and zero hours Designing, the total of the 4Ds (45+14+1+0) equals sixty hours. To get your Do-

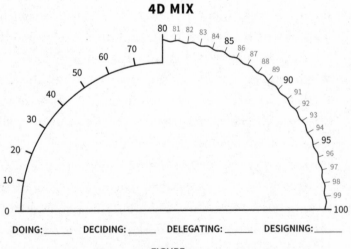

4D MIX

DOING:_____   DECIDING: _____   DELEGATING: _____   DESIGNING:_____

FIGURE 5

ing percentage, divide forty-five hours by sixty hours to get 0.75, meaning 75 percent. Continuing the example, Deciding is 23 percent, Delegating is 2 percent (both with rounding), and Designing is 0 percent. With the percentages calculated, fill in each D category at the bottom of the graph.

6. As the final step in the analysis, fill in the "pie wedges" for each D to represent the proper percentages in the graph (the 4D Mix). The wedges will show the distribution of your work types (the 4Ds). You can also download this on the resources page at Clockwork.life.

While each work type is necessary, many businesses are unbalanced. We will look at the entire business later, but for now let's start by just looking at where you stand. And again, if you are a solopreneur or have a small business of five employees or fewer, either you *are* the business or you are a major part of the business. What do you notice? What are your realizations?

Many solopreneurs fall into the trap of having 95 percent or more of their time allocated to Doing. They are living in a time-for-money trap—the Survival Trap—where the only way to grow is by Doing more, but you can't, because there is no time.

I've also seen solopreneurs trap themselves in a Design-heavy 4D Mix. Putting 40 percent of your time in Designing (which is way more than the optimal 10 percent) may indicate you are a dreamer, but it surely means you aren't spending enough time Doing the work to turn those dreams into reality.

Warning! Since we analyzed only five days of your life, you may have analyzed a week where, for example, you were doing a quarterly tacking plan. I detail the tacking strategy in my book *The Toilet Paper Entrepreneur*, but the core essence is simple: tacking is a quarterly protocol where you observe the market around you and the influence it may have on your overarching goals, and then adjust your business strategy to realign with your Big Beautiful Audacious Noble Goal.

If you do your time analysis during a tacking (i.e., planning) period, your analysis is not representative of your typical allocation of time. Here is the deal: you can and should trust yourself. You know what your typical workweek is like, because it is the workweek that you live. So you have permission to go back to step 1 and write down what you think is a typical week.

The optimal 4D Mix, of course, works for multi-employee companies. For example, if you have two employees (you being one of them), the average of both your individual 4D Mixes constitutes your company mix. So, if your 4D is 50 percent Doing, 0 percent Deciding, 0 percent Delegating, and 50 percent Designing, and the other employee's is 80 percent Doing, 20 percent Deciding, 0 percent Delegating, and 0 percent Designing, it is the average of each category that gets you your business mix.

(Note: I realize you may work seventy hours a week and your employee forty hours a week, and therefore more emphasis should be put on your percentages. But that level of detail does not do much at all to impact the results, so let's not get that nitty-gritty. Plus, our goal is to reduce your time from seventy hours and get it way down. Remember?)

In this example, the company's mix is 65 percent Doing (the average of 50 percent and 80 percent), 10 percent Deciding (average of 0 percent and 20 percent), 0 percent Delegating (average of 0 percent and 0 percent), and 25 percent Designing (average of 50 percent and 0 percent). So this business is 65/10/0/25. Compare that with the optimal 4D Mix of 80/2/8/10, and we can see we need to ramp up the Doing (getting things done) and reduce the Deciding for others (perhaps we outsourced to virtual help, and they need way too much direction). There is no Delegation going on, and we want about 8 percent of the time spent on empowering others to drive outcomes. Twenty-five percent of the time between these two people is spent on the Designing (vision and future thinking) of the business, which is too much (it should be around 10 percent).

If you have a large company with dozens, hundreds, or thousands of employees, you can still do this exercise for everyone. But do it in groups by department and responsibilities. For example, say you have two hundred employees, and your accounting department has ten people. Have each person in the accounting department do a 4D Mix analysis. Then average out across the department. Now you will have the 4D for your accounting department. Do the same for other departments and then create charts for each department. Add up the department 4D Mixes to see what your company 4D Mix is.

START WITH 1 PERCENT

I realize the shift I'm asking you to work toward can seem overwhelming, especially if, at the moment, you can't imagine how you'd free up *any* time to focus on Designing your business. This is why, as you begin this process, I'm asking you to set aside just 1 percent of your work time for Designing. If you work forty hours a week, that's twenty-four minutes a week, rounded up to a half hour. If working sixty hours a week is closer to your reality, that can be rounded to just one hour of Design time. You don't even have to block off an entire hour (or whatever your 1 percent equivalent is) for Design work; you can break up the time.

With even 1 percent Design time, you can focus on optimizing your 4D Mix and other strategies to help you streamline your business. You know what else you'll be able to do? You'll finally be able to pick up that folder of "someday" ideas you keep in the drawer and figure out if you still want to pursue them. The articles about industry trends and new technologies you've been meaning to read, the video trainings you've paid for and haven't yet watched—you can use your 1 percent time to finally get around to doing that important research. Even with just thirty minutes a week, you'll have time to do one of the most important analyses of your business: ask what is working and find ways to do more of it, and ask what is not working and find ways to do less of that.

Once you get in the habit of setting aside the time, you'll become more comfortable taking the time—and making good use of that time. You'll start to see changes in your attitude toward your business, and changes *in* your business as you begin to implement some of the ideas and strategies you came up with during Design time. And once you get used to taking Design time as a matter of course, you'll want more of it.

YES, YOU CAN MAKE ANY BUSINESS RUN JUST LIKE CLOCKWORK

If you're a creative entrepreneur, or an entrepreneur with a special skill set on which your business depends, how do you shift from Doing to Designing? I get this question from time to time. It's important to remember that Doing, Deciding, and even Delegating maintain your business. Designing *elevates* your business. And even if you are in an industry as specialized and independent as painting, you can be the designer of the business. Don't believe me? I'll let Peter explain.

Seventeenth-century German artist Sir Peter Lely was certainly not the first artist to systematize his art, but he was arguably the first to make his company run like a well-oiled cuckoo clock. (See what I did there?) Lely painted in the Baroque style that was popular at the time. After he moved to London, he quickly became the most sought-after portrait artist and then the "Principal Painter" for the royal family. He was best known for a series of ten portraits of ladies of the court—the "Windsor Beauties"—that hung in Windsor Castle.

His work in high demand, Lely opened a workshop and trained other painters to help him complete his paintings. This fella didn't just have a few assistants; he had a massive operation that allowed him to do what he was known for, what he did best: paint faces, leaving the rest of the portrait to his assistants. When customers wanted some of that "Windsor Beauty" magic, it was all about the face. But if Lely painted every portrait in its entirety, including the subject's attire and surroundings, he would be spending the majority of his time working outside his zone of genius, i.e., capturing faces. If he stayed in the Doing, Designing, and Delegating phases exclusively, the only way he could scale was to work harder and longer.

So, jumping right into the Designing phase (while never fully abandoning the other phase), Lely sketched a variety of poses and numbered them. He often used the same dress design and the same props. After he finished a subject's face, his lead artist would assign someone on the team of artists to use a template for the numbered pose required and paint the rest of the painting. Cleary, Lely was the Godfather of paint by numbers.

Business boomed because he delivered on the one thing his clients wanted most: Lely's interpretation of their face. The rest—the setting, the color of the dress, the props used—didn't matter much. And because he was able to focus his Doing solely on painting faces and Delegate the rest, he was able to turn out thousands of paintings over his lifetime while his contemporaries were lucky to turn out a hundred.

The next time you dare to say "my business can't be stream-lined" or "I need to do all the work," take a pause. You are lying to yourself. Your business can run on its own. If an old-school painter can do it, you surely can, too.

For the longest time, I struggled with the idea that, in my business, others could do the core work or, from my lips to God's ears, *all* the work. My enemy was my ego. I believed I was the smartest person in the room—at least when it came to my business. But it all changed when my friend Mike Agugliaro told me about a simple change he and his partner made. Mike and his business partner, Rob Zadotti, grew a plumbing business from the days of the two of them racing around in a beat-up truck to a $30 million home-service business. How did Mike make the shift from Doing to Designing a world-class business (which was ac-quired in the summer of 2017 for, as Rob put it, "a sick amount of cash on the barrelhead")? They did it by changing the ques-tion they asked. They no longer asked, "How do I get the plumb-ing work done?" Instead, they asked, "*Who* will get the plumbing work done?" That simple change of question started to bring the answers that made them business designers. For you to become your business's designer, you can no longer ask "how," but "who." That one question, "*Who* will get the work done?" will open your eyes to a business that will cruise right to the design phase.

I can't tell you how many times entrepreneurs say to me, "My business is too unique. It can't be systematized." Sorry to break it to those people, but they're not that special. Yes, they have a few things that are special to them, but 90 percent of their business is the same as everyone else's. So is mine. So is yours.

Few businesses in the world are that unique. And when they truly are unique (and successful doing it), everyone else copies them. Say goodbye to the uniqueness. Now don't get your undies in a bunch. Your mom was right, you are special and different and all that. I'm just saying the business fundamentals stay constant for all businesses. Since you're reading this book, I'm going to assume that you are at least willing to put your ego aside and attempt to run your business using the Clockwork system.

The best part is, streamlining your business doesn't take a ridiculous amount of work to build a bunch of new systems. In fact, it is ridiculously *easy* when you realize that *you already have all the systems*. The goal is to simply extract them from where they are already documented—in your head. You'll learn how to do that in chapter five. And when we do that, you will be free to do what you do best. Whatever work you do, it can be broken down into steps and delegated to someone else.

And if you don't want to give up too much of the Doing because that's what you love? Then by all means, do what you love. Your business should make you happy. The point is, you *can* delegate more than you realize. Even if your business is a work of art.

OPERATION VACATION

At the start of the chapter, I told you the first part of Scott and Elise Grice's story. Elise spent a total of six weeks in the hospital, totally unable to work on her business. Most of us cannot imagine taking six hours off from business, let alone six weeks. It's not just entrepreneurs. Employees are taking less and less vacation time. A 2017 study[*] showed that of US employees who are eligible to take paid time off, only about 50 percent of them actually do it.

---

[*] Harris poll on behalf of *Glassdoor*: Amy Elisa Jackson, "We Just Can't Unplug: 2 in 3 Employees Report Working While on Vacation," May 24, 2017. www.glassdoor .com/blog/vacation-realities-2017/.

And, no surprise, two out of three US employees who *do* take vacation time end up working for at least part of their vacation. It's not just an entrepreneurs' issue—it's part of our work culture.

But what if you were forced to take the time off?

In our conversation that day, Elise said, "We're thankful for my stay in the hospital because it was a turning point for us. That day when everything seemed hopeless, we decided to wipe the slate clean and ask different questions. Instead of asking ourselves 'How are we going to get through this?' we asked the question 'If we could be paid to do anything in the world, what would we want to do?' We were at rock bottom, and that actually freed us up to *ask* that question."

I can relate to rock-bottom freedom all too well. I am sure you have heard the popular question about discovering your passion and purpose: "If you had all the money in the world, what work would you do?" It is a great question, but it has bias built into it. It suggests that whatever you choose does not need to offer sustainability. You could say, "I would watch *Curb Your Enthusiasm* reruns morning to night," and since you have a continuous stream of cash, your Larry David binge would be a fine choice. The goal of course is to find an activity that satisfies you and is not trumped by the need to make money.

I have discovered a second, rarely asked question that is equally important, and works in concert with the first: "If you had no money at all, what work would you want to do to support yourself?" When the answer to both questions is the same, you have found your direction. That is how I found my life's passion of being an author. I had fantasized about being an author "one day" when I asked myself the "if I had all the money in the world" question, but I never pulled the trigger. When I nearly bankrupted myself (and my family), I was forced to ask the question "What do I want to do, now that I have no money?" The answer was the same. I wanted to be the most prolific small-business author of this century. Same answer and my path was clear.

While only time will determine whether I achieve my Big Beautiful Audacious Noble Goal—being the most prolific small-business author—the journey has been the closest to experiencing heaven on earth. I love what I do. Elise and Scott loved branding, and they wanted to scale their business, but they couldn't pull that off with their established business model. And they wanted something different, something more.

Elise said, "Before I got sick, I had been slipping Scott little 'I quit' Post-it notes, mostly because my role in the business was very confrontational. I routinely had to tell our clients they were wrong about their branding, and I didn't want to do that anymore. I really just wanted to get paid to go to coffee with people."

Scott's answer was rooted in his passion for business systems: "I wanted people to experience freedom in their personal lives because of their business."

When Elise started to get better, they scaled back their team, finished their client work, paid off their hospital debt, and began building a business with a new model that would allow them personal satisfaction and freedom. They shifted their business model to focus on delivering training and content to groups rather than to individual clients. They no longer managed client projects; through online classes, they began advising their former clients, new students, and followers how to manage their own projects. Though they weren't aware of the term at the time, they successfully balanced their company's 4D Mix. Within seven weeks, they had created a streamlined business that educated their existing clientele—and a new, growing client base—about branding and business systemization through online courses.

Today, Elise and Scott run their business from a twenty-eight-foot camper van. They regularly take four- and six-week vacations from their business, vacations where they are completely out of the day-to-day operations. And what happens to their business when they're away? It grows and grows.

"Last summer, we both took three months off from our business and traveled through Europe together," Elise said. "We completely checked out. No social media. We didn't write a newsletter. Didn't answer one email. We built our business so that, if we wanted to take a break, our business would still grow. We streamlined the entire process. And when we came back from Europe, we had more business and more revenue than we had before we left."

Elise and Scott did something critical to bring operational efficiency: they stopped doing what they didn't like doing. They didn't just delegate it; they restructured their entire business so they no longer did things that they didn't like to do and only did the things they liked. Then they sought out ways to do what they wanted with the flexibility they wanted. Where you stand in your business is a direct result of your thoughts about what you need to do to be where you are. If you believe you need to work your ass off to grow, you will prove yourself right. If you believe you can make your business scale with little effort, you will prove yourself. But it only happens if you believe it can happen. And the only way to come to believe it can happen is to start asking empowering questions. Just like Scott did. Just like Elise did.

In my own quest to develop a simple way to make my own business run on automatic, I've met several other people who took sabbaticals from their business only to come back to a more successful business than when they left it—including one person who left for two entire years! I'll share more of those stories with you throughout the book. Hearing their stories made me realize that taking a long vacation was the best test for a streamlined business, and committing to *taking* that vacation is the best incentive to streamline your business in preparation for that vacation.

Then I had an epiphany: Committing to a four-week vacation—the length of most business cycles—is the perfect incentive to streamline your business. During a four-week period most businesses will pay bills, market to prospects, sell to clients, manage payroll, do the accounting, take care of administrative tasks, maintain technology, deliver services, ship products, etc. If we know we're going to be away for four weeks without access to our business, we'll do whatever it takes to get it ready for our absence. If we don't commit to the vacation, we'll take our own sweet time getting through the streamlining steps, and since we're humans, we'll probably stop before it offers us any lasting relief. The ego is strong, and the grind is all-consuming. And the draw of the all-too-familiar grind, painful as it is, is the easier choice to make, simply because it is familiar. Without the forced goal, we may never do this.

With this book, I'm launching Operation Vacation. You and I and everyone, we're all in this together, and we can support one another in taking the steps we need to take to grow our businesses *and* get our lives back. *My challenge to you is to commit to taking a four-week vacation sometime in the next eighteen months.* And when I say commit, I mean book that vacation. And to make sure you never back out of it, tell your kids, tell your mom, write it in your diary. Or, make the boldest declaration of all: post it on Facebook so the world will be up your butt if you don't do it. No matter what, make sure you email me your commitment (I'll tell you how in a second). Maybe we will end up on vacation at the same time in the same place. We can throw back a margarita while your business grows in your absence.

In chapter ten, I give you a detailed, step-by-step timeline that will help you get your business ready for your four-week vacation. If you're a rebel, or a nonbeliever, and you have already decided *not* to take a four-week vacation at some point in the next couple of years, please read the chapter anyway. The timeline provides a framework for clockworking your business using seven steps.

Let me clarify that I am not suggesting that you can *only* take a four-week vacation. For some people, four weeks may seem too short. Or, if you're thinking about having a baby, you may want to take three to six months off, or more, and you may not have a clue how you're going to pull that off while keeping your business alive. That's why we are going to *plan* to take a four-week vacation, so we can get your business running itself. Once that happens, you can take as much or as little time off as you want or need to do. Imagine that—you may not have to put off major life decisions in order to keep your business running and growing!

As I am writing this book, I too have committed to taking my very first continuous monthlong vacation in December 2018. To be exact, the trip will start on December 7 and end on January 7. I started the plan for the monthlong sabbatical eighteen months prior, and have already run multiple one-week tests away from my business to prove that it is ready. And throughout these eighteen months, I have been thinking about my business in a whole new way. Knowing this trip is coming, I am focused on removing myself from all critical roles. I'm working toward the optimal 4D Mix. Would I have done that without forcing the issue? No, I think not. And I don't think you would have, either.

As my extraordinary business coach, Barry Kaplan of Shift 180, says, "Sometimes the only way out of the weeds, Mike, is to simply get out of the weeds."

That's it. Stop spending all the time contemplating how to get out of the weeds. What if things don't go as planned? What if the business collapses? What if? What if? Just get out of the weeds and then measure the results. Book that vacation now! Get outta Dodge (which ironically is known for its voluminous amounts of weeds). The moment you are solid on your trip, your mind will shift and you can get to work on moving yourself to the Designing phase of your business.

 ## CLOCKWORK IN ACTION

1. It's time for you to get some Design time. In *Profit First*, I implored readers to commit to setting aside a minimum of 1 percent of their revenue for profit. Even if they didn't follow any of the other steps in the book, I knew that the action of taking 1 percent profit would accomplish two things: They would discover how easy it was to set aside that money, and they would learn to live without it. For this action step, I'd like you to set aside 1 percent of your work time to focus on Designing your business. Just 1 percent. No matter how big your to-do list or how demanding your customers and staff, your business can survive you taking a tiny amount of time each week to do the work that will help your business move forward.

2. Block out this time, every week, for the next eighteen months on your calendar. As you move along, you will be expanding the amount of Design time, but for now, you and I just need to ensure that 1 percent is protected for a long time.

3. Just as you need to take your profit first in your business, you need to allocate this 1 percent of time first in your week. Don't wait for the end of the week to do the design work. Instead, allocate the time right at the beginning. By working on the vision at the start of the week, the rest of the week will naturally support that vision, therefore getting you to it faster. Run the time analysis on yourself for the next five business days, and determine your 4D Mix.

CHAPTER THREE

STEP TWO: DECLARE YOUR COMPANY'S QUEEN BEE ROLE

How do you shift your business toward the ideal 4D Mix? How do you start the process of making your business more efficient? I started looking for solutions for my business four years ago with a simple question: What is the most efficient organization in the world? That is what we all aspire to have—an efficient organization that generates money on automatic, which, in turn, gives us the freedom to do what we want, when we want. My Google result? Squat-o-la.

It would be awesome if answers to our most burning business questions were readily available on the internet. Sorting through pie-in-the-sky theories, listicles, and definitions makes it impossible to find proven solutions. It's kind of like shaking a Magic 8-Ball to gain deep insights. Not going to happen! Still, I was desperate. I'm sure you've done it yourself, typed in "how do I make my business stop stressing the living crud out of me?" or something more colorful. And Google responds with a recipe for sugar-free, gluten-free, taste-free muffins. Which, in the greatest irony of all, makes you more stressed . . . I mean, if you take the sugar and gluten out of a muffin, all you are left with is air. And that paper doily thing.

With not much luck on Google, I hit the library. (Yes, they still exist.) Books, research papers, and articles that explain the systems used by specific companies abound: how this shoe manufacturer produces more sneakers in less time, how that distributor sped up its shipping process, how Disney succeeds using "The Disney Way."

I was sure that someone, somewhere, had a list of "the most efficient businesses," and I wanted to study how they became efficient and translate what they did into practical advice I could use and give to you. The problem was, the businesses that turned up in my research always seemed to have captured lightning in a bottle. They simply figured out what *they* needed, not what *we* needed. And that's not replicable. After all, you've never been to Disney #2 or drank a Coca-Cola #2, have you? You can compete, just like Six Flags or Pepsi does, but you can't just copy another business verbatim and expect identical results.

Then, one fateful day during a long drive, I flipped through radio stations and came across the most random report about bees. An NPR field reporter was out there with a beekeeper, reporting on how these insects do the amazing work they do. And, in typical NPR fashion, they shared some of the live action, including a sting that the reporter took when he got a tad too close to the hive.

As I listened, what impressed me most about bee colonies was their ability to scale extremely fast and nearly effortlessly. You may have seen it for yourself. A bee buzzes around outside your window one day, and what seems like the next day, you spot a massive hive there. How do bees do it?

Each bee in the colony knows it needs to do just two things, in the same order, every time. First, each bee must ensure that the queen bee is protected—nothing is more important, because of the role she serves. Then, and only then, the bees go do their Primary Job. As a result, their buzzness (I swear I will only do that once) grows quickly and easily.

Here's how bee colonies operate:

1. A hive has a queen bee, and her role is to lay eggs. The task of laying eggs is the Queen Bee Role—the QBR. If the QBR is humming along, eggs are laid and the colony is positioned to grow fast and easily. If the queen bee is not fulfilling her role of laying eggs, the entire hive is in jeopardy.

2. Every bee knows the most critical function for the colony to thrive is the production of eggs, so the queen bee, who is designated to fulfill that role, is protected and served. She is fed. She is sheltered. She is not distracted by anything other than doing her job.

3. Don't confuse the queen bee as being the most important part of a colony; it is the role she serves that is most important. Eggs need to be made quickly and continually. One specific queen or another is not critical; the QBR is what is critical. So if the queen bee dies or is failing to produce eggs, the colony will immediately get to work spawning another queen bee so the QBR can get going again.

4. Whenever the bees are satisfied that the QBR is being fully served, they go off to do their Primary Job. Which could be collecting pollen and nectar (food), caring for the eggs and larvae, maintaining the hive temperature, or defending the hive . . . from being exploited by NPR reporters.

After learning how beehives scale so efficiently, I had the *aha* moment of a lifetime. I realized that declaring and serving the QBR would radically improve any entrepreneur's business, and an entrepreneur's quality of life. I decided to immediately test my theory in my own business—more about that later—and with Cyndi Thomason, an entrepreneur I had been coaching, one-on-one, in recent years.

If you read my book *Surge*, you might remember Cyndi's story. In brief, I guided her through the Surge growth process; she followed it to the letter, and, in just a couple of months, went from one marginal lead a month to one solid lead a day. Her business *exploded*. She was now in the uncharted territory of having to turn away new prospects left and right. It was an amazing transformation; she now had better and better clients and better and better profits. It also sucked; Cyndi had more work than ever before. She was beyond overwhelmed. She was in full-on panic mode. She worked constantly, and it still wasn't enough to keep up with the demand.

Cyndi has this comforting Arkansan accent, and she's a great orator. Kind of like a female version of Bill Clinton. Except the day she told me about how overwhelmed she was, she sounded like Bill Clinton in a Barbara Walters interview, talking through tears.

When I asked her what her QBR was, Cyndi wasn't able to come up with an instant answer. We discussed it, and eventually she was able to land on her company's core function: compassionate and clear communication. Cyndi said, "When I speak with my clients, no matter what is going on, good or bad, I find a way to make them understand the circumstances and bring them back to a state of confidence. I give them peace of mind. For us, that communication keeps everything on track."

When Cyndi wasn't checking in with her clients, taking the

time to understand their concerns and clearly explain solutions, she saw a noticeable decrease in income. When she did, revenue increased. Communication, she had decided, was critical to the success of her business.

Just as laying eggs is the QBR for bee colonies, proactively communicating with clients is the QBR Cyndi identified for her company. What single action does your business hinge its success on? That's your QBR. Don't worry if you don't know off the top of your head. I have a super-simple, yet powerful, exercise coming up shortly that will reveal it for you.

"How much time are you spending on the QBR [checking in with your clients] in a forty-hour week?" I asked Cyndi.

There was a long pause. Not one where the person is trying to compute the answer. But one of those pauses where the answer immediately came to mind and the person is playing out the implications of their answer. Cyndi then spoke up. "Maybe two hours."

Two hours out of forty. Five percent! Five percent of her time was spent on the most important role in her business. And let's be honest, Cyndi doesn't cap her workweek at forty hours. (Neither do you.) She is spending less than 5 percent of her time on the QBR. And the other 95 percent of the time, Cyndi was busy doing the books, managing employees—you know the drill. Even with more employees, her work did not get easier; it intensified. She had more people doing stuff for her . . . effectively more hands. But Cyndi was still stuck in making every decision. Her job was one of two things at any given time: relentlessly doing the work or answering the never-ending stream of questions from the people who were supposed to be doing the work for her. Her business was one brain (hers) with eight arms (theirs) flailing all about. As a result, her business growth actually put *more* stress on her. Sound familiar?

Once we identified Cyndi's QBR, we made the shift. She had one goal: protect the QBR at all costs. She made her team aware of just how critical the QBR (communication with clients) was. She even put up a giant peace sign in her office as a visual reminder for all that the QBR is to bring tranquility, understanding, and peace of mind to their clients. She then transferred non-QBR work away from herself and to her assistant, employees, and contractors. She pushed decisions down to her employees. And then she focused on doing the QBR work. And when she identified the last big distraction from doing the QBR work—her personal management of a large, albeit problem, client who could never be satisfied . . . she fired them.

Three months later, I checked in with Cyndi. "I can't believe it," she said. "We are growing faster than ever, and the business is running smoothly. And guess what?"

"I'm all ears, sister."

"Last week, I *gardened*. All weekend."

Cyndi *loves* to garden. It's her passion, and because she was so overwhelmed by her business, she had lost that. Identifying and declaring her QBR naturally brought her closer to the optimal 4D Mix. Now, with her focus on streamlining—using the methods discovered in bee colonies, and that you will discover as you continue through this book—Cyndi got her weekends back. She got her *life* back, and her business is thriving.

IDENTIFY AND DECLARE YOUR QUEEN BEE ROLE: THE STICKY NOTE METHOD

If you haven't already figured out your QBR from the basic direction I've given you so far, here's a great method to use to identify it. Even if you have a pretty good idea of what it is, the following method is a great way to validate the QBR. The sticky note method works by zeroing in on the most critical thing that any individual is doing for the company. This method can be used to declare the company's QBR and to declare the most important thing each employee does in their role. It's best to do this exercise in a group, if you can, since it can spark powerful realizations and conversations. If you're a one-person band, *es no problema, mi amigo.*

We are going to back our way into the QBR through deductive reasoning. We will first start with all the different major tasks being served by your employees (including yourself) in your company. Once we determine the Primary Job of each employee, we will analyze those to determine which is the company's QBR.

1. To get started, gather your team and grab a few sticky notes for everyone. In fact, grab a lot of 'em, since each person—including you—will need at least six. Have each person spread out the notes in front of them. Remember, if you are a one-person band, you can just do this by yourself. The rest of the instructions are written for each person at the table to follow from their own perspective, regarding their own job.

2. On each sticky note, write one of the six most important things you do in your job. Of all the things you do for your company in a day, a week, a month, or a year, what are the six big things that matter most? Keep it short. You don't need long sentences. For example, you might have a sticky note that reads "sales" or "invoicing."

3. With the six sticky notes displayed in a line in front of you, look at each one and confirm that it represents, to the best of your immediate thoughts, one of the six most important things you do for your company. In the top

left corner of each sticky note, jot down the approximate time you spend doing that thing.

4. Now pretend that you are no longer permitted to do two of those things. The game is this: you will never be able to do these things again, nor can they be delegated or transferred to someone else. Once these things are removed, they effectively disappear (for this exercise). Take the two sticky notes away and put them aside, out of your immediate sight. This exercise will not be easy. But don't let it discourage you; the result of completing this process is eye-opening.

5. The four remaining sticky notes should be what you consider the most important. While you look at the remaining notes, imagine ways that you can elevate the degree of that work so effectively that it would cover for the permanent loss of the other two functions that you just removed. Explain to the group why you removed those two sticky notes. If you are doing this process solo, just talk to yourself. No one notices nowadays anyway.

6. Now delete just one more. The consideration is identical. One thing must go and can never be returned. Add it to the two other sticky notes you put aside. Explain why you removed this one and why the others stayed.

7. Now, with only three sticky notes left, remove one more. Follow the same process as you have been, narrowing down to the two elements on which you would be most willing to hinge your job's success.

8. In the final step, you are left with two sticky notes. Rather than remove one, choose which of the two on which you will take your stand. Choose the one thing that is so important it can never be removed. It will never go away. It is the one thing on which you would be most willing to

hinge your success. Explain to the group why this contribution is more important than all of the others. This is what I call "the one for the wallet"—the task that must always be done. The task that must be protected at all costs. In your work, that is your Primary Job. Put that sticky note in your wallet and never forget it and never forget to do it. The Primary Job takes precedence over all other tasks . . . unless the company's QBR is in trouble, in which case you will revert to protect and serve it.

9. Keep all the sticky notes from the exercise, even the ones you put aside! We'll need them for an upcoming chapter.

First, all employees go through this for their own work (that includes you). In their capacity, what are the six most important things they do for the business? The one for the wallet is the task they see themselves doing that most helps the business move forward. This is what they see as their Primary Job at your company. The one most critical role they serve, secondary to only one thing. Let's say it together: protecting the QBR.

When each employee announces their Primary Job, if it is inconsistent with what you believe is their number one role, you have a communication or congruency issue. Either they don't understand your expectation or you don't understand their role. In a case of inconsistency, work with that employee to understand the incongruence.

Once you have identified the primary function of each employee, as the owner of the business, you collect their one remaining sticky note. If you have fifteen employees, including yourself, you should have fifteen sticky notes. We are now going to use these fifteen sticky notes to repeat the exercise for your company as a whole. You may notice you have some duplicates among these fifteen. Perhaps multiple people have identified a sales function or a deliverable they create as their Primary Job. In this case, consolidate those notes by sticking them together and get to the *distinct* Primary Jobs and lay them in front of you.

Start removing sticky notes by first cutting the quantity in half. So if you had, for example, twelve sticky notes left after you consolidated down from fifteen, you would want to remove six sticky notes (half the notes) and put them aside. Keep halving the group that remains until you get to four or fewer remaining. Since you have six now, halve that into three. Three go to the pile you have put aside, and three remain. Then, once you have four or fewer in front of you, take them off the pile one at a time.

It often happens at this point that people say this "game" is impossible. For example, of the three notes you have left: invoicing, delivering a service, and direct marketing, you cannot remove any more since it seems they are all necessary for the business to survive. Invoicing is essential, and so is delivering the work you promised and getting the word out. I agree, they are all essential, but the question is, on which one of these functions would you hinge your business success? If you don't pick the one thing, you will continue to dilute your business's uniqueness and cripple its ability to run on automatic.

You must select one as the priority over everything else. So imagine you permanently remove invoicing by putting it aside in that pile. The question is: Can you then elevate your marketing so effectively and do it so well that prospects gladly pay you in advance without ever being invoiced? Can you market so well that you never need to invoice? Can you market so well you can hinge your business success on it? The answer is a big "hellz yeah." Kickstarter campaigns prove this is possible every day.

Of your remaining four or fewer sticky notes, keep removing one at a time until you get to the one thing. That's your company's QBR. That's the one for *everyone's* wallet.

Here is the super hint to help you identify your QBR: For most small businesses, the role is most often served by the owner or the most expensive employee(s). And as a critical reminder, it is *not* the owner or the employee themselves. It is the *role* they serve. We are talking about the Queen Bee Role here, emphasis on "role." We are not talking about the queen bee . . . yet.

I need to repeat a few words of caution: Most entrepreneurs automatically assume that they are the QBR, but this is key: The QBR is *never* a person, or machine, for that matter. It is always a role, a function, or a task. So while you may be fulfilling the QBR right now, and perhaps are even the only person serving the QBR, that doesn't mean it always has to be you. In fact, it shouldn't.

If you are the owner of a small business of five or fewer employees, the QBR is likely being served by you. If you are a solopreneur, it absolutely is being served by you. And if you have a larger organization, it is often (but not always) served by your most skilled people.

Let's talk about my friend Jesse Cole. The Savannah Bananas baseball team is arguably among the most remarkable teams in all of baseball—majors, minors, college—all of them. And not because it is a great team with great players. In fact, the players are all-star college kids who rotate every season. The team is constantly changing, and many of the fans don't know the name of a single player on the team. Why? Because extraordinary baseball is not the Bananas' QBR; extraordinary *entertainment* is.

As Jesse puts it, "Baseball is just the break between the entertainment." And the entertainment must always be fresh. I mean, imagine watching your kid's soccer game twenty weekends in a row; that would get draining. Wait a second, you already lived that. Their first game is fun. But when it starts repeating, it becomes somewhere between boring and frustrating. Just kick the damn ball, instead of picking daisies in the field. Just kick, kid. Just kick!

Jesse knows baseball is even worse. Everyone is just standing around waiting for someone to hit a ball, and in this case your kid isn't even out there. So Jesse set the QBR to new fresh entertainment. Anything and everything gets stale. As a result, Jesse is constantly cooking up new ideas for crazy stunts the support staff can perform and fun games the fans can play in between innings.

Jesse invited me to throw out the opening pitch at a game this past summer in front of five thousand Bananas fans. What an honor! Except it wasn't a baseball; I threw out a roll of toilet paper (in honor of my book *The Toilet Paper Entrepreneur*) and the crowd went wild: it was fresh, fun, silly entertainment. QBR served. For the Savannah Bananas, the QBR is served not by Jesse alone, but by everyone who entertains the crowd. And for that one game, for that one opening pitch of toilet paper, the QBR— for a few seconds—was served by me.

A couple of years ago, I met my friend Clyde and his wife, Bettina,* for dinner in Frankfurt, Germany. Clyde and I have been good friends for years, but this was my first chance to get to know Bettina. Over dinner, I discovered that she was one of fewer than fifteen hundred physicians in the United States who is licensed and board certified to practice pediatrics in an intensive care unit. To get to that point, she'd completed eleven years of school and training.

---

* To protect their privacy, Clyde and Bettina are *not* their real names. Sadly, their story is all too real. Should you be curious about how I came up with their names, it was simple. I asked them what names they would never have wanted their parents to give them when they were born. The answer was Clyde and Bettina. So there you have it, meet Clyde and Bettina.

CLOCKWORK

For most of us entrepreneurs, eleven years of higher education seems like forever and a day, but equate it with the early years of running your business. Or if you're an employee who happens to be reading this book, equate it with the time you put in getting an education, training, and learning your industry from an entry-level position. Just as Bettina invested time and money into her career, you've invested time and money into your business.

Like us, Bettina was passionate about her work. Extremely so. She loved working with the most critical pediatric patients in the city she lived and worked in, and she loved teaching attending physicians. She even loved the research she was expected to do in her free time. The only problem was that she knew she wouldn't be able to sustain it for much longer. She already had multiple years in the industry as a doctor, and with the relentless volume and variety of demands put on her, she figured she would be lucky if she made it ten years. Cumulatively.

Imagine this: You have five twelve-hour shifts, followed by a thirty-hour shift. In addition to patient care, you have training and mentoring related to your professorship. Then add two to three hours of patient and administrative documentation. Then pile on top of that billing and dealing with insurance company disputes. After your shifts, you have more admin work related to teaching interns. Then, when you miraculously have the energy to pull an unpaid all-nighter, you have to write research papers so that you can get promoted, if you're lucky—a few years from now. You're so exhausted you need to invent a new word for exhaustion, one that probably rhymes with "please help me."

"I love my job, but I just don't think I'll be able to keep this level of intensity and maintain mental and physical health," Bettina told me. "I had to come to grips with the fact that I won't be a full-time practicing physician my entire life. And I'm not the only one. Ten years seems to be the burnout rate for physicians at the hospital where I work."

It blew my mind that Bettina, who was an elite physician with specialized training, training that patients desperately need, had to come to terms with the fact that, unless something changed dramatically, she couldn't stay in her position for much longer. It blew her mind, too. She is just entering her prime, yet she is in such drain pain that she is about to tap out.

"You plan for the eleven years of additional schooling, but no one tells you how the workload will affect you. It was a big shock, knowing how much time and money I've spent on my training. I just can't keep up this level of intensity and stay healthy and sane, and I have to be okay with that decision."

Bettina is being forced to change her life plan, and the hospital is losing one of its best doctors because it has set up a never-ending work flow—aside from patient care—that cannot be sustained. Would giving Bettina a productivity hack help to reduce her stress? No, because the hospital already has given her dozens of them, and with her "free time" it quickly finds a dozen new ways to fill it up with more work, with things like insurance claim disputes. Imagine that? You're having life-saving heart surgery and your surgeon takes a break in the middle of the operation so that he can argue with an insurance agent why he used ten stitches during the last operation instead of the insurance-mandated three.

You know the saying "Don't busy the quarterback with passing out the Gatorade"? This is because the QBR is so important. The quarterback has a job to do. He has got to move that ball down the field, not dole out drinks to rehydrate his teammates. Similarly, Bettina shouldn't be bothered with tasks that interfere with serving the QBR. It's so obvious that it is hiding in plain sight. Bettina needs to save lives first, last, and all the time in between, yet she is often stuck passing out Gatorade. It's more than just a shame; it's a sin.

And it's a sin if you don't cherish the QBR, either. In the next chapter, I'll tell you how to make sure you and your team empower *your* quarterback—whoever is serving the QBR—to get that ball down the field and all the way into the end zone, with a "hokie" touchdown dance and all.

CLOCKWORK IN ACTION

I have only one action step for you: Identify and declare your QBR and who is serving it.

Yes, that's it. If you have a small team, this exercise should take you less than thirty minutes to complete. If you have a big team, you may have to set aside a day to finish it or break the team into groups. But this process is critical, so please do it. Your company's success hinges on it. Plus, once you declare your QBR, you will start to find your way out of the weeds and begin the process of becoming the designer you need to be. The QBR is the linchpin to a business designed to run itself.

CHAPTER FOUR

STEP THREE: PROTECT AND SERVE THE QBR

W hen your seven-year-old has a shard of metal in his eye, the twenty-two-minute drive to the Cape Cod Hospital emergency room is the easy part. The father, a trained emergency medical technician (EMT), knows the hard part is what's coming. As painful as it is, his son's condition is not life threatening, so they have a wait in front of them. A long, uncomfortable wait.

It's a warm day in June, and the waiting room is packed with people. A siren outside grows louder as an ambulance approaches. The whimpering boy and his father settle in for a long day and night in the ER.

It does not go as they expected.

Rather than a holding tank, the ER is more like a busy beehive. Within five minutes, not only has the boy been admitted, he is receiving treatment. Fourteen minutes in, the shard has been removed using a special magnet and the boy's eye has been thoroughly reexamined by a doctor to make sure it is free of any permanent damage. At nineteen minutes, the final check has been completed, the Tylenol prescription has been written, and the boy is released. Sixty minutes after they left for the hospital, the father ushers his son through the front door of their vacation home. All is well. The vacation is back on track.

That same day, 256 miles away in Brooklyn, two EMTs bring a mentally ill forty-nine-year-old woman suffering from agitation and psychosis to the Kings County Hospital Center. The waiting room is packed. Five minutes later, the woman is sitting on a chair in the ER's waiting room. Fourteen minutes in, she's still waiting. Nineteen minutes after her arrival, still waiting. One hour. Four hours. Eight hours. Ten. The patient is still waiting, still sitting in the same chair. *Twenty-four hours* later, she is found dead on the waiting-room floor.

It was June 18, 2008, and the little boy who was back home within an hour of arriving at the ER was my nephew, Dorian. The woman who died tragically in the ER after a full day of waiting was Esmin Green. The cause of death was pulmonary thromboembolism, which are blood clots that form in the legs and work their way through the bloodstream to the lungs. And how did Ms. Green get the blood clots? The medical examiner concluded that the clots were due to "deep venous thrombosis of lower extremities due to physical inactivity." In other words, she was *sitting too long.* Twenty-four hours too long. While Dorian was running on the beach, his eye healing and his brief experience in Cape Cod Hospital's ER already a fading memory, Ms. Green was still waiting for medical attention—scratch that; she was *dying* for medical attention.

When I discovered that Esmin Green was admitted to an ER on the same day as my nephew and met a tragic end, I knew I had to share the story with you. If you've read my other books or heard me speak, you know this story isn't one I would typically tell—no jokes to break the tension in this tale. Systems are a serious matter. When they work, they bring freedom. When systems fail, the outcome can be deadly.

When I first heard the two parallel stories, they didn't compute. Cape Cod serves a smaller population than Brooklyn. Cape Cod couldn't have the same equipment that Kings County had. (They didn't.) But the police report* regarding Ms. Green's death is revealing. The systems and the accountability were deadly horrible at Kings County Hospital. There is no question that systems played a central role in creating both outcomes. One hospital knew the key to moving patients quickly through the process, and the other hospital did not. Or, if it knew, it didn't follow it.

What went wrong at Kings County Hospital Center that tragic day in 2008? They may claim an overcrowded waiting room, but Cape Cod Hospital also had a full waiting room that day. They may claim that they did everything within protocol. But I would bet serious coin that the reason Kings County failed and Cape Cod succeeded is that one protected the QBR and the other probably didn't even know it existed. Cape Cod knows exactly what its QBR is—though they don't call it that—and they do everything they can to protect it. Kings County Hospital Center may not know or care to know its QBR, and if they don't know (or care), they can't actively protect it.

In an emergency room, the QBR is very likely the role of diagnosing an emergency medical issue and determining the proper course of action. That is a role that only the doctors (and sometimes physician assistants) can do. The ER can see a patient through to resolution only when the doctor has availability to see a patient. If the doctor is not available, patients are forced to wait

---

* www1.nyc.gov/assets/doi/downloads/pdf/pr_esmingreen_finalrpt.pdf

and then wait longer in a room designed specifically for one purpose—to allow people to wait even longer. Welcome to the purgatory of the waiting room, where all good intentions for organizational efficiency go to die. But if the QBR is fully served, all elements of the ER start to flow again. The waiting room empties out and patient after patient gets the medical attention required. But this only happens when the QBR is defended and the person (or people) serving the QBR is protected.

To make sure the QBR is protected, a well-run ER makes sure the doctors who serve the QBR do nothing but identify the medical issue and prescribe a course of action. If a doctor is filing papers, directing staff, or idly waiting on the patient to be assigned a room, he or she is not protected, and therefore the QBR itself is not protected. An unprotected QBR can result in dire consequences. In operating like an efficient beehive, the support staff must make sure that the QBR is running unabated, and that every other task, no matter how small or how big, no matter how important or insignificant, no matter how urgent or trivial, is handled by someone other than a doctor.

Running a business can feel like a life-or-death situation, especially when you're overworked, overwhelmed, and overly tired. Sometimes it *is* a life-or-death situation—tragedies happen in many different industries. Really, though most of us aren't dealing with ER-level drama in our businesses. Seven-day workweeks, demanding clients, employees who come to us for every little thing—these are the dramas most of us face. Still, while we may not have to worry about our companies causing a sudden death, the relentless stream of demand on us does cause a slow death. A slow, soul-sucking death. A death of passion for our business. A death of drive. A death of happiness. But that can all be turned around quickly and easily for any business. Two hospitals had two very different outcomes. Not because they are in a different business, but because one understood the path to the highest levels of efficiency and the other didn't.

That's why, once you've identified the QBR, everyone else on your team must prioritize protecting the QBR so that the role can be fulfilled. Then, and only then, can they focus on their Primary Job.

The number one goal for you, and for everyone on your team, is to protect the QBR so that the QBR can drive the business forward without distraction or interruption. That's it. That's the main goal. That's the one thing that will make your business skyrocket to organizational efficiency. Protect the QBR. Always.

The strategies in this chapter will help you create a plan for protecting the QBR. You don't need to knock it out of the park with your QBR protection plan on day one. You just need to get started with it, and notice the impact it starts to have. That will get the momentum going. As you and your team work to protect your QBR, your 4D percentages will naturally shift toward your target.

ALL HANDS ON DECK

Normally, I'd shift to a new concept next or explain it in a different way. But I want to tell you one more story first. Mrs. Wilkes' Dining Room in Savannah arguably has the best family-style Southern cooking in Georgia, perhaps the world. It's a great place to visit before you head off to a Savannah Bananas evening game. Mrs. Wilkes' feels like two dozen of the world's best grandmother cooks whipped up their favorite dishes for their family dinner, but instead of plopping it down on the dining room table, they scootered it over to the fabled Savannah restaurant. The food is that good.

In 1943, Mrs. Sema Wilkes took over a boardinghouse in historic downtown Savannah with the goal of making the area's best Southern meals. The QBR was obvious: food that is remarkably delicious. The result speaks for itself. The typical line waiting to get in the restaurant is one and a half to two hours. People start to line up hours before the place opens, not just on a holiday or vacation week, but every day.

The job of the staff, just like yours needs to be, is to protect and serve the QBR. Every employee plays a role in either directly serving the QBR or protecting the QBR. The chef and team in the kitchen are directly serving the QBR by gathering the finest and freshest local ingredients. The rest of the team is protecting the QBR. The serving staff makes sure that when you arrive at your table the food is ready to go. They actually serve the table *before* you get seated. Food is rotated quickly to keep it warm and fresh. If a table's food delivery is slow, another staff member will jump on it. Everyone knows what they are known for. And their job is to make sure the food is top shelf. Everyone's job is to make sure the most important role of the business is protected, and everyone contributes to it in some fashion, either by complementing it or by stepping in when necessary, or both.

The servers exude Southern hospitality. The restaurant is basic, but spotless. The ambience is very much family oriented; you better be ready to meet strangers because you will surely be sitting with them at the large tables that seat ten people. And when you are finished, you will be carrying your plates to the kitchen to be cleaned. Great food, good service, and fun times. All those things are necessary to keep you in the restaurant business, but you stand out on your QBR. If the food wasn't exquisite, the restaurant would be more of a gimmicky place.

Sema Wilkes passed away in 2001. Her granddaughter runs the restaurant now, and she maintains strong relationships with the local farmers, ensuring top ingredients. The granddaughter knows that their business's success hinges on serving the QBR, not Sema herself. And while Sema is sorely missed by all who loved and knew her, the QBR is served unabated. If the kitchen needs a hand with prep work, one of the serving staff will immediately take on the role. The entire staff helps with preparation and gives feedback if there is any problem. Is the chicken slightly dry? If a dish is even just a little off from perfection, the staff rushes that input back to the kitchen. It almost never happens, but it could, and the team knows the food, the QBR, is everything.

Protect and serve the QBR as though your life depends on it, and your business becomes the "must go there" for customers, just like Mrs. Wilkes' Dining Room is for foodies. People travel the world to go there and consistently rave about the experience. And, if you didn't know, Mrs. Wilkes' is only open three hours a day, Monday through Friday. The place is packed. Always.

EXERCISE: HUB AND SPOKE

If you haven't figured this out by now, the person or people serving your QBR are probably spending too much time doing everything *but* serving the QBR. Likewise, your other employees are also spending too much time doing other things when they could be protecting the QBR and serving their own Primary Job. And they are probably, although with good intentions, actually detracting from the QBR and their Primary Job.

In this simple exercise, you and your team will be able to clearly see how focused you are on serving or protecting the QBR, doing your Primary Job, and how distracted you are by other tasks. Then you will know which tasks the person(s) serving the QBR needs to offload to someone else, which tasks need to be automated, and which tasks need to be dumped.

To get the hang of it, do this analysis on yourself first. Then do it for each person who is or should be serving the QBR (you may likely be one of them). Then do it for the rest of your staff, where the center of their paper is their Primary Job. This is not only fun, it's eye-opening.

1. On a blank sheet of paper, write the QBR in the center and draw a circle around it, like a bull's-eye. Remember, we identified the QBR in the last chapter using the sticky note exercise. You did that, right? If not, go back and complete that immediately. I'll wait.

2. Look at the five other sticky notes you created—the ones that ultimately were not your QBR—and the time you spend on each task during any given week. You can pull the data about time allocation from the Time Analysis you did in chapter two. Review how much time you spend on each of these five tasks, and get a sense for how they compare with one another, so that you can draw a spoke radiating out from the QBR equating to that time.

3. Now draw a hub-and-spoke chart. The QBR is the hub, and tasks are placed in boxes around it. Each task's distance (the spoke) from the QBR represents the time it takes. For example, a task that takes ten hours a week would have a spoke that is five times longer than a task that takes two hours a week.

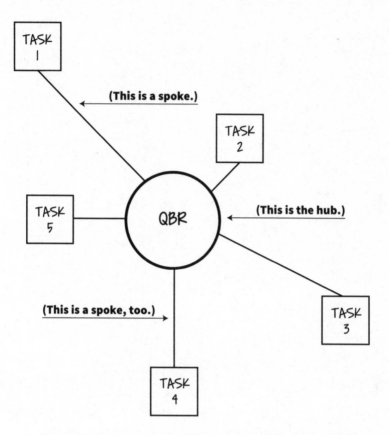

Now, beside the diagram, jot down all of the additional work you do in your weekly routine that you don't already have drawn in the hub-and-spoke diagram. You can easily do this by pulling data from the Time Analysis you completed. The additional list of work may include: responding to email, making sales calls, meeting with employees, answering questions, sending out bills, cleaning the office, responding to even more emails. Write it all down. The goal is not perfection here. Just write down what comes to mind and don't go crazy with detail. At most, list ten new things. If there is nothing to add, that is absolutely fine, too.

TASKS	TIME
Answer Questions	4 hrs
Invoicing	2 hrs
Email	8 hrs
Sales Calls	7 hrs
Internal Meeting	1 hr

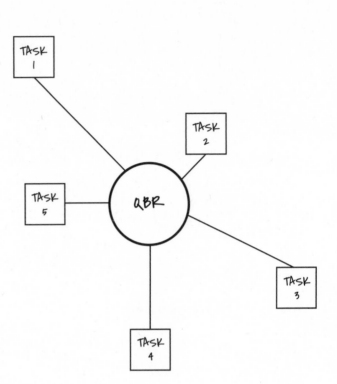

4. Then write down the approximate time per week you spend on each of the tasks you just added to the chart. You can pull this data from the Time Analysis exercise.

5. Now add to your hub-and-spoke diagram the additional tasks you wrote on the side. Look at your diagram (see the example on page 82). It is likely unbalanced with some long spokes and some short. The spokes are a great visual to see how far each task takes you away from serving your QBR. Do you see that? Do you feel the pain?

6. **Trash, Transfer, or Trim:** Now, starting with the tasks that are the furthest away from the QBR, determine for each whether you can trash it, transfer it to someone else (delegate), or trim it. For example, you might trash writing a daily update email that no one on your team seems to

read (or need), transfer social media management to a freelancer who specializes in that area, and trim your "introductory free consults" from one hour to thirty minutes.

One common task that can be trimmed *and* transferred is answering questions. Most businesses get the same twenty or thirty questions from customers over and over again. Assign (transfer) someone the responsibility to respond to those questions and then delegate the task of creating a FAQ that will save them from having to answer each question as it comes up. Create an email response that reads: "Thanks for your question. This is a recurring inquiry, and I have created a FAQ that answers your question, as well as thirty others we get regularly. Click here."

Whomever you transfer those necessary but distracting tasks to—another person on your staff or a freelancer—will be protecting the QBR by taking care of them and ensuring they don't come back on your plate. Plus, when you transfer a task to someone else, their job is to take ownership of it and trim it themselves (possibly with some of your strategic input and experience). The sooner we get these activities off your plate, the faster you will be able to devote more time to serving the QBR. Trimming the task means you have to keep doing it because you are the only one capable, but you're going to find a way to limit how much time you spend doing it.

There may be some tasks that only you can do in the near future and must stay with you, or may have such a strong contingency with the QBR that it needs to stay linked (for now). For example, you may have a contractual obligation to a client to be the point of contact for an active project; you'll have to finish this before you can trans-

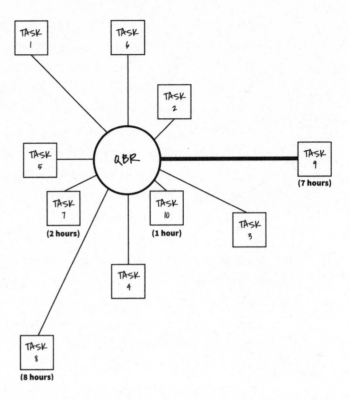

Answer Questions	4 hrs
Invoicing	2 hrs
Email	8 hrs
Sales Calls	7 hrs
Internal Meeting	1 hr

fer this type of work to another team member for future contracts. Darken that line from the QBR to the task.

7. Cross out any tasks that can be trashed on the hub and spoke chart, and stop doing them immediately. Put arrows over any tasks that you can transfer, signifying that they are leaving your realm of responsibility in short order, and get busy delegating them. And put a squiggly line through anything left that you can trim (meaning you still will do the work for now, but it can be done more efficiently). Darken the lines of anything that you absolutely must do (except for the QBR). You may have to keep doing those dark lines and those squiggly lines for now, but it isn't sustainable for the long term if you want to have a business

TASKS	TIME
Answer Questions	4 hrs
Invoicing	2 hrs
Email	8 hrs
Sales Calls	7 hrs
Internal Meeting	1 hr

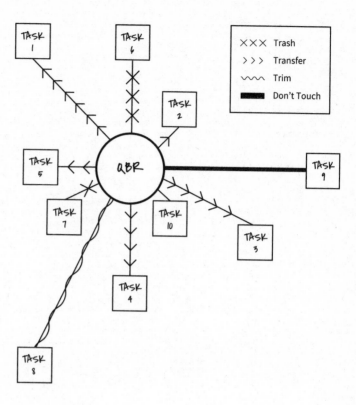

that can run like clockwork without you. Ultimately, we'll even take the QBR off your plate (the goal is to get you from Doing to Designing, remember?), but we can't pull the trigger on that one just yet.

8. Keep going through the QBR hub-and-spoke model, working your way closer and closer to the QBR. You need to move as many tasks as possible into trash, transfer, or trim. All the time you recover in the process should immediately be reserved for further serving the QBR. As you put this into action, you'll see that elevating the QBR dramatically elevates your entire business.

Please visit Clockwork.life for a video that shows this process in action.

TASKS	TIME
~~Answer Questions~~	~~4 hrs~~
~~Invoicing~~	~~2 hrs~~
Email	~~8 hrs~~
Sales Calls	7 hrs
Internal Meeting	1 hr

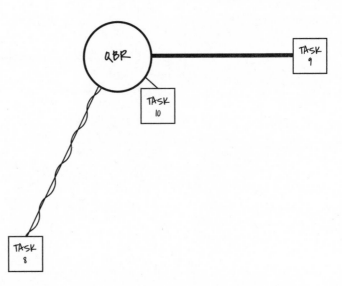

Once you've completed this exercise for yourself, repeat the hub-and-spoke exercise across your organization, applying trash, transfer, and trim to every task that your colleagues do, using the sticky notes from chapter three as a starting point. Use the trash, transfer, and trim method to ensure that each of your employees is dedicating the maximum amount of time toward doing the job that creates the biggest impact on the business.

WHAT DO I TRASH, TRANSFER, AND TRIM?

As you go through this exercise, what do you do if you encounter tasks that are transferable, but there isn't anyone to transfer them *to*? That is often a signal to make a hire.

As we transfer work away from the QBR and away from the Primary Job, you will see that less skilled tasks are the first ones to be transferred. This typically means you can employ less expensive people or part-timers/freelancers for that work. The goal is to have a few expensive skilled team members at your business, focused almost exclusively on doing the most skilled work, and transferring all the other necessary, but easy, repeating tasks down the skill chain. That's a streamlined business. And that is exactly what the trash, transfer, or trim method supports. Now, let's get busy doing it in your business.

First, evaluate a task and determine whether you can trash it. Does it support a necessary objective of the business? Does it add measurable value to your clients or to your team? You see, not everything is necessary in a business. In fact, many tasks that may have been necessary at one time are no longer necessary but hang around because "that is what we've always done." Trash the things that are not necessary. And if you are unsure, just stop it for a period of time to see if there are consequences. No consequence = not needed. Trash it.

Next, seek to transfer work to other people or systems that will free you and your expert people to take on bigger, more challenging tasks. Transfer work down to the most inexpensive resources and empower the new owner(s) of the task to achieve the intended outcome more efficiently. In other words, have them trim it.

For the stuff you must keep, evaluate how it can be trimmed. Can an existing task be done faster or more easily? Can the cost of materials and time associated with this task be reduced? If a task can't be trashed or transferred, it can still often be trimmed. Seek ways to reduce the time and costs of completing a task while achieving the necessary results.

THE HUB AND SPOKE IN ACTION

Let me take you through the hub and spoke exercise and how it could work for a fictitious online retailer that ships the coolest jeans on the planet. We'll call it Cool Beans Jeans LLC. Using the sticky note exercise, we have determined that the work of designing the coolest jeans on the planet is the QBR, that function on which Cool Beans Jeans hinges its success. Remember, once we declare the QBR, our goal is to serve and protect it fully. We do this by creating systems to free the people who are serving the QBR from having to do anything that would ever make the QBR secondary. In the center of the paper, we write the QBR and draw a circle around it. This is the hub. For Cool Beans Jeans, the QBR is "breathtaking design."

1. List the people who currently are serving the QBR, part-time and full-time, and those who should be doing so but are spending next to no time on it. Following this process, we will analyze everyone on the team. Each person will do the sticky note process and get their own blank sheet with the QBR in the middle.

   In our example we identify the founder and lead innovative designer of Cool Bean Jeans, former rapper Fat Daddy Fat Back. Fat Daddy* is the sole designer for Cool Beans Jeans. (You may be the Fat Daddy in your company, or maybe you serve a different role.) There are four other employees, but Fat Daddy is the sole jeans designer.

2. In this case, the QBR is being served by a single person. But it can often be a group of people or even a machine or computer that is serving the QBR. Write the name of this person or thing at the top of the paper. So Fat Daddy's name goes up top.

3. Since we are assuming Daddy Fats (that's his given name) has already done the sticky note exercise, all those other tasks are added as spokes to the QBR hub.

4. Then he adds the list of all the other tasks he does. This is tricky for Fat Daddy because he always just does stuff and never really thinks about what he is doing. For now, he writes it down to the best of his recollection. Later, he may do a Time Analysis (you can do this, too), which looks like this:

---

* If you are a fan of the Profit First Podcast, first, thank you. Second, you may remember the episode when Ruby Tan started calling me Fat Daddy Fat Back. My new rapper name stuck so well that a website just may have sprung up as a result. And the website just might be FatDaddyFatBack.com. And I might, just might, be Eminem's doppelgänger.

TASKS	TIME
Shipping	3
Internal Training	1
Photographs	5
Marketing Campaigns	10

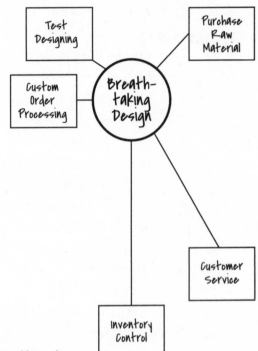

Note: Chart does not show all of Fat Daddy's tasks.

5. Fat Daddy spends sixty-five hours a week working in his business. He spends about five hours a week serving the QBR. In other words, five hours a week is spent elevating the business (designing incredible jeans) and sixty hours a week he is actually doing stuff that keeps the business down (not designing incredible jeans). It is hard to believe, since he thinks "everything is equally important." But that is not true. The other things are necessary (perhaps) but not critically important. All those things must become secondary to the QBR. To do that, we need to get them off Fat Daddy's plate, and that is done by picking

TASKS	TIME
Shipping	3
Internal Training	1
Photographs	5
Marketing Campaigns	10

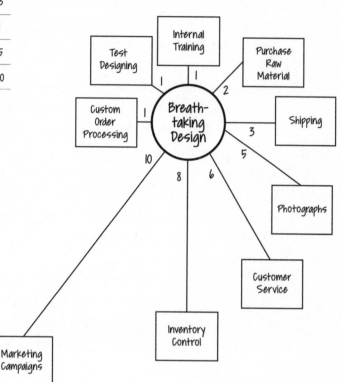

them off one at a time: trash, transfer, or trim. To make it visual, Fat Daddy draws the hub-and-spoke diagram, with the length of the spokes representing the time he spends on each task. Next to the line going to the task, he writes the distance (time) it takes him away from the QBR.

6. Fat Daddy first analyzes the task that takes him the furthest away from his QBR. If it is easy or at least easy enough to delegate, he starts there, by delegating it to another employee. The goal is to get a quick win under his belt in the name of delegation, so the tasks that are the easiest to delegate and will have the biggest impact

in protecting the QBR should be addressed first. Fat Daddy draws arrows on the items to be transferred and assigns them permanently. He is also very aware that some things he does are not even necessary. Fat Daddy trashes those things fast by crossing them off the chart.

7. The task taking Fat Daddy furthest from the QBR is implementing the marketing campaigns, so that is the first thing he will transfer to someone else. And he knows the perfect person to do it . . . Zil Aksnirbod.* Zil loves marketing and knows what the customers love. Time to delegate. That will bring ten more hours a week to work on the QBR—designing incredible jeans. Fat Daddy draws an arrow over that task and gets to work on bringing Zil up to speed.

8. Fat Daddy pins the chart next to his desk. As he trains Zil on this new responsibility, he makes it clear to her what this will do for the QBR and that her job is to first and foremost ensure that he is able to focus on the QBR, since this is the secret sauce that elevates the entire company. As Fat Daddy moves on to do more QBR work, Zil's Primary Job is to fully run the marketing. She will report in the staff meetings and keep him abreast, but she needs to make the decisions that will move the jeans out the door.

9. Fat Daddy also realizes that shipping the jeans himself is not such a great money saver. Just like having a doctor run around handling the filing for the office, he is using an expensive resource (himself) to do inexpensive work. This is a big indicator that the QBR is not being pro-

---

* I have had a one-person marketing team ever since I became an author, more than ten years ago. She is nothing short of extraordinary. Her name is Liz Dobrinska and I can't speak more highly of her. For those with a sharp eye, you will notice that Fat Daddy Fat Back's best marketer is Zil Aksnirbod (Liz Dobrinska spelled backward). Wow! This is like a Sherlock Holmes novel . . . secret clues everywhere.

tected. Whenever expensive resources are doing the inexpensive work, the balance is surely off. Immediately transfer the work. Even if you are a microbusiness of one, as soon as humanly possible, get that inexpensive work off your plate and go focus on the big, impactful stuff. Hire a part-time assistant, get an intern, pull Mom or Dad out of retirement and let them volunteer to help. Just get help fast. The longer you do the inexpensive work, the longer your business will be trapped in inefficiency, and as a result will stay tiny forever.

    a. Fat Daddy does a basic value analysis. A world-class designer like him easily makes $150,000 a year. Divide that by two thousand work hours a year, and you'll get $75/hour. He completes ten shipments of jeans an hour. Meaning, each shipment costs the company an additional $7.50 (the cost of his time per shipment). He could hire an intern for $10/hour and now each shipment cost goes down to $1. But better yet, he captures three more hours a week to do the QBR. The intern is hired!

    b. Photographing the jeans also seems like a potential money saver. He spends five hours a week on it, and his cost to his company is $75/hour. A world-class photographer bills $150/hour. On an hour-to-hour cost rate, Fat Daddy is the less expensive choice, but additional considerations come into play. Looking further, a pro photographer will get *all* the work done in two hours, it will be lit properly, and the photographer's work will be website ready. A little cheaper to get done, way better photos, and, most important, another five hours for the QBR. No-brainer.

TASKS	TIME
Shipping	3
Internal Training	1
Photographs	5
Marketing Campaigns	10

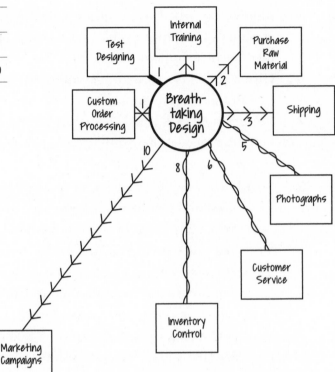

10. Now Fat Daddy identifies the things that he "absolutely" has to do because it requires a skill that is so untrainable that he just has to be the guy (for now). He feels that testing the designs really needs to be his responsibility, since the results influence his design (the QBR). So, the only "only for me" task besides the QBR is testing designs. He darkens the line to that task, to identify that it needs to stick with him for now. The only things he will do going forward is serve the QBR and the one other task. The rest will be delegated or dumped.

11. As each item is transferred it gets crossed out and more time goes to the QBR. It takes time, but Fat Daddy gets more and more time to make breathtaking designs. His jeans are so amazing and so cool, the celebrities want them. People go crazy over them. The business leaps forward, because the QBR is being served.

WHEN YOU'RE THE ONE WHO SERVES THE QBR

What if it really seems as though you're the only one who serves the QBR? The objective is simple—get others serving the QBR.

Remember Cyndi Thomason's story? After following the Surge methods for rapid niche-based growth, her business grew so fast she became overwhelmed and exhausted. Having more demand than you can serve (right now) is a good problem to have, but it is exhausting. We did the sticky note exercise and she found her QBR: communication with clients. She then did the hub-and-spoke diagram and removed the tasks that took her away from the QBR. Then, she immediately set about freeing herself from serving the QBR by getting her team to serve it themselves.

Cyndi defined what great communication with clients was. Cyndi determined ways to measure how frequently and how well communications with clients was happening. And then she started tasking employees with doing the QBR, too. They knew that the QBR had to be protected, and since they were the ones serving it, they now had a simple rule: When multiple things are pulling for your time and attention, always prioritize the QBR over everything else.

The demand on Cyndi's time plummeted and her company's efficiency jumped. That may sound totally counterintuitive, but it is exactly the result you should experience when you focus on the QBR. Let me repeat it one more time: The demand on Cyndi's time plummeted *and* her company's efficiency skyrocketed. Boom!

Sometimes, you'll have to let go of your role serving the QBR. The QBR at Vitality Med Spa and Plastic Surgery Center is its development of cutting-edge processes in keeping its patients looking and feeling young, fit, and healthy. Maybe it's obvious; maybe it's not. The clientele commit to major procedures, such as weight-loss therapy, plastic surgery, Botox applications, and discreet matters, such as vaginal rejuvenation. There is a lot of complexity to some of these, so the perfection of the operations is a necessity. The founder of Vitality Med Spa, Monique Hicks, empowered her team to protect and serve the QBR in many ways, including one unique "trick." More on that in a minute.

I first met Monique in the fall of 2017 and was blown away by what she had accomplished. She had grown Vitality Med Spa to a $3 million-plus operation while raising a daughter as a single parent. She recounted how for the first three years of business she exclusively served the role of the QBR. She was researching procedures and working hand in hand with clients to make everything perfect for them. She swooped in like a superhero when problems arose. She did everything to protect and serve the QBR, by herself.

Monique explained, "Then one day it became very clear the business was dependent exclusively on me. The energy and effort I brought to the business was what customers were getting out of it. I realized the business was only as strong as I was on any particular day. It was exhausting and not scalable. That's when I taught my team about how I was serving my QBR, which I had been calling my 'zone of genius,' and how I needed them to protect and serve me in that role."

The teaching part was easy. Monique had one-on-one meetings with each employee, explaining how to customize experiences for customers, learn about their individual needs, and specify the optimal procedures. She used a daily huddle to highlight how people were making both big and small improvements, and empowered employees to learn from one another. She had employees share best practices.

Monique also showed respect for the employees' domain. Even though in the past she "swooped" in to fix things, employees sometimes interpreted it as interference. With clarity on how to protect and serve the QBR, Monique stopped swooping in and employees felt more confident in the service they were providing. Morale increased. Things got better—for the most part.

There was just one problem: Monique was the only one doing the QBR work. Her employees weren't coming to her with ways to further improve the company and their services, even though they were the ones doing the work.

Remember that unique trick I alluded to earlier? It was a special hire Monique made. The QBR is the essence of the business and is the responsibility of all the employees to protect and serve in some capacity. Even when—especially when—the boss is failing to protect and serve the QBR.

Monique is human, like all of us, and is prone to mistakes. And she is the first to admit that she isn't always sure on how to improve or change the company's services. She realized that, even at times when she slipped up and failed to do the QBR work, employees would notice but not say anything. The employees had a hard time speaking up to Monique, because they were too timid or couldn't believe a company existed where the quality of the service was more important than even the boss's opinion. Monique saw the blockage in the communication lines and took a unique measure. She hired a "strong-voiced" individual who wasn't intimidated by Monique in any way. The new hire was put in charge of day-to-day operations, collected "frontline feedback" from staff, and would sit with Monique to discuss the feedback, uncomfortable as some of it was. The company leaped forward in quality of service, and continues to grow accordingly.

"The QBR is an all-in commitment, Mike," Monique shared with me. "The team needs to know it and act upon it. And if either is not happening, it is the owner's fault. Their inability or fear of being honest with me about the QBR was not their problem, it was mine. So I set out to fix it immediately."

WHEN THE QUEEN WANTS TO STAY QUEEN

Even the most exciting, profitable, and popular businesses can be dependent on one person. When you achieve success, meet your personal goals for impacting the world, and love what you're doing, it can be difficult to see how pulling yourself out of the equation would make any sense. Some entrepreneurs derive so much joy from serving their QBR that they want to keep doing it indefinitely. Motivational speaker and king of the infomercial Tony Robbins has chosen to continue in his role serving the QBR for his business. So have other uber-successful experts, such as my pal Marie Forleo.

Marie has a massive fan base. I'm talking millions of raving fans. She has a thriving business and is living her mission—and she has structured her business so that she can take tons of time off and still grow it every year. She is basically living the Clockwork dream.

Her business goes dark for two weeks every summer and winter—everyone is off. It's part of her company culture. "There's nothing in our business that is life or death," Marie says. "And our customers love it, because it inspires them to emulate us in their own businesses. My customers and my colleagues replicate what we do.

"For my team, it's really the best thing. Everyone works really, really hard. They are dedicated and driven. To have everyone off at the same time, nobody feels like they're missing out, nobody feels like projects are moving ahead without them. They can all just recharge. Some of them cry with gratitude, because they've never experienced the working environment we've created here."

I first heard about Marie from my readers. In fact, many of my readers tell me, "Marie Forleo is da bomb!" She is the founder of what she calls a "socially conscious digital empire," which includes B-School, a training system for entrepreneurs, and MarieTV, a weekly program broadcast in 195 countries that helps entrepreneurs create a business and a life they love.

When Marie started out in this industry, she was twenty-three, was working as a bartender, and saw one-on-one coaching clients on the side. Today, her B-School has more than forty thousand graduates from 130 countries, across 160 industries. She has approximately twenty full-time employees, and when B-School is in session, she will also expand with seasonal and part-time people as needed. Compare this to a college that may graduate five thousand students a year, but has seven hundred employees! Talk about running a tight ship!

One of Marie's intentions is to make the biggest amount of impact on the most people. Millions, in fact. That is her Big Beautiful Audacious Noble Goal. Over the years, she has streamlined her business to meet this goal while also meeting her personal goals of living a balanced life *offline.* For example, she used to run a major conference in New York for three hundred attendees. When she assessed the impact vs. the work involved and compared it to B-School, she decided to simplify and kill the conference—as well as every other revenue stream, including highly profitable private business coaching. Making this shift more than doubled her business.

"It's still a lot of work, but it's deeply, deeply satisfying. I'm most excited about helping people unlock their full potential. It's so much more fulfilling to have less things you focus on and do really, really well," she told me. "Also, it puts us way ahead of the competition."

Marie's QBR is creating content, and her team protects her time so she can stay in the creative space. That content pulls in new subscribers and fans and, hopefully, customers. It educates and inspires people to fulfill their dreams, which fulfills Marie's mission on this planet. And the free content is also a marketing tool for B-School.

Still, with the exception of editing her content, Marie is the only person who serves the QBR. On the outside, it looks as if she *is* the QBR. But if Marie wanted to replace herself so her business could grow without her, she'd have to train other people to create content without her. Maybe she doesn't want to do that, though. It's clearly her zone of genius, and she gets so much satisfaction creating content that serves her base. She is out to change the world, and she's doing it.

Marie has made a conscious choice in continuing to serve the QBR. I wanted to share her story because you may elect to make the same choice. Countless others choose to serve the QBR alone. It works, and it can be extremely rewarding, as Marie is experiencing, but I want you to be aware of the trade-offs. The day Tony Robbins, or Marie Forleo, or you (if you decide to solely serve the QBR) decide to call it quits, the business quits. When you decide to slow down, the business will slow down. When you are the sole server of the QBR, you are the heart of the organization. From my conversations with Marie, it is clear she is extraordinarily successful and takes extraordinary joy in what she does. She is *very* aware that she is the heart of the company, and she is comfortable doing it for now.

As we said goodbye she said, "I get so much energy out of my work, it would actually hurt me to stop doing it. The day will come when I am ready for the business to live and grow beyond me, and that is when I will find others to serve the heart of the business. But for now, I'm not changing a thing. I think I will have a million graduates of B-School first."

The choice is yours, and I am surely not here to make it for you. Trust your instincts, but know your options. When you serve the QBR, you are the heart of the organization. When you choose to have others serve the QBR, you become the soul of the organization.

CLOCKWORK IN ACTION

1. Now it is time to clear the plates for the people serving the QBR. Take the easiest and most distracting thing off their plate. Even if it's just one thing, the impact can be huge.

2. Consider how your team is working currently. Do you have your most skilled people doing unskilled work? If so, that approach is costing you. Use the trash, transfer, and trim method to move work to the appropriate people. Usually you will find most of a company's work is highly repeatable and requires little skill. An army of interns or part-timers, and subsequently fewer highly skilled (expensive) people, may get more work done, faster, better, and cheaper.

3. Once you've taken steps to ensure that the QBR is being protected and served, it's time to make a choice. Do you want to be the heart of the business and do the QBR work yourself, or do you want to be the soul of the organization and have others serve the QBR? If you choose the latter, you need to take another simple step. How? We'll get into that in the next chapter.

CHAPTER FIVE

STEP FOUR: CAPTURE SYSTEMS

The loud voice echoed though the office. "Create systems? I don't even have time to get the work done, and now I have to create this detailed step-by-step document? We don't need systems; we just get things done. I just do the stuff. My people just do the stuff. Jeeeez." That outburst was mine. Just a moment of weakness as I struggled to transfer low-value tasks to my intern.

Creating systems takes a lot of time! Doesn't it? At least I thought it did, and you may feel the same way, too. The idea of creating systems so that whoever is serving the QBR (or doing a Primary Job) can offload other tasks is overwhelming. It is extraordinarily time consuming. And it is often a waste of time because by the time the system is fully documented, it is no longer relevant. First, we must think about the outcome we need to create, then figure out a step-by-step sequence to get there, and then document it. Soon—no, strike that—much, much later, as in many moons later, we have a shelf full of three-ring binders representing our systems: best practices, workflow guidelines, chains of command, and more. Blood, sweat, tears, late nights with coffee, and early mornings with tequila went into those binders, and does anyone ever really use them? I mean, does anyone ever really use them for something other than kindling? I think not.

I used to think this laborious process, as painful as it is, was necessary. I'd done it dozens of times in the past, never with any success, mind you. But nothing else worked, either, so after I tried and failed to roll out yet another system, I would attempt to eradicate my frustration by doing the process "just one more time." And my frustration grew . . . like a boil . . . a gross, monster-sized boil only seen in sci-fi movies (or on an especially unfortunate teenager).

I remember doing this for used book shipments. I had discovered a great marketing and money-making opportunity in used books and decided to streamline the entire process. I easily spent four hours creating a step-by-step standard operating procedure (SOP). The final document was a fifteen-step recipe with each step written simply and clearly, complemented by pictures. When the masterpiece was done, I gave it to my intern and she got to work. Problems ensued.

First, the document was not perfect. As she went step by step, there were variables I forgot and steps I had inadvertently skipped, which threw her off. In minutes, she was back in my office with questions, which put me right back into the Deciding phase. She had the hands to do stuff, but I was the sole decision maker for all the arms. You know the Indian goddess Kali? She has many arms, but only one head to control them all.

I updated the SOP to fix what I had missed, and soon found I had missed more. Then there were anomalies. What if the order was expedited shipping? What if the order came in on a weekend? What if, God forbid, the customer ordered two books? Do we ship them separately or together?

Before, I just used my judgment to do whatever made sense in the moment, but now I was committed to turning this into a document that could handle anything. The SOP expanded to address anomalies. I spent more time developing it. More going back and forth. And then all hell broke loose: the U.S. Postal Service updated its website. Every picture and step that was documented in the SOP about the shipping process needed to be redone. And in the midst of all that, Amazon changed *its* backend system, too. *Ugh.* The hours and hours, and days and days it took to document one simple procedure was all out the window. I couldn't even make one SOP foolproof, let alone the hundreds that I would need to create for my business. It just wasn't worth it. The thought of doing this for my entire company had me thinking that death by hara-kiri (the infamous Japanese suicide ritual) was a more appealing option.

People are like rivers. We will seek the easiest path to get where we are going. And when you see your employees ignoring your SOPs, that is a sure sign the SOPs aren't working. The goal of every organization should be to seek constant efficiency and improvement. Waste of materials, waste of money, and waste of time are the bane of every business and must be addressed constantly. Traditional SOPs don't seem to serve that goal anymore.

Of the thousands of entrepreneurs I have worked with, a minuscule few have active documented systems. I also don't have such a system, not in the traditional sense. And when I visit an entrepreneur's office and ask to see their SOPs, there is usually nothing but a mix of documents and emails that are buried away on some virtual cloud drive that no one can find.

What most companies do is on-the-job training. In technical words: "We are just going to wing this puppy." Whatever they tell you to do, do. And when someone else tells you to do something else, do that. And if those directions conflict with each other, just do the best you can to serve both, and make sure you teach the next person that.

This process may sound familiar. After all, it is wired into the fabric of humanity all the way back to caveman communications. Since they didn't have much of a written language, cavemen drew pictures on cave walls and told stories to one another around the campfire, about things like how to make a campfire.

One caveman would tell the clan, "Ugh. Strike rocks. Bigger rocks make bigger spark. Make sure cavewoman sees your rocks, if you know what I mean. Ha. Ugh. Ha. Ha. Ugh." Stories go from one caveman to another, and like the telephone game you played as a child, the original message turns into something else. "Strike rocks" may morph into "Spike fox," and those goons are off to poke animals with sticks, and when they get back, no one knows how to start a damn fire.

To make sure the QBR is humming along, and that your company is operating at the optimal 4D Mix, you'll need to systematize both the QBR and everything else around it. The whole goal of an SOP is to have a consistent process to produce a consistent outcome. But SOPs are really hard to make, since you don't have the systems yet. And they are super hard to maintain, since things change constantly. There has to be a better way—and there is.

Since you, the business owner, are very often the "queen" in this scenario, freeing you is necessary to ensure your business is not dependent on you. It will give you the ultimate freedom that right now may only seem like a pipe dream, but is really quite doable.

YOU ALREADY HAVE SYSTEMS

First, let me clear up the most common misconception about systems right off the bat. You may be thinking, "I don't have any systems," or something like "I need to create systems from scratch." Wrong. So wrong! You, in fact, have every single system for your business already. Every single stinking thing. All of your systems are in your head and/or the heads of your employees. All those tasks that you need to delegate are already being done by you. You already follow a process, in your head. So you don't need to create anything new. Nor do you need to painstakingly extract them, step by step, from your head onto paper. The goal is not to create systems; the goal is to capture systems—and do it easily. This is how you transfer the knowledge of tasks and get your business to run like clockwork. The best part is anyone can do this and it is ridiculously easy. First, let's get the method that *doesn't* work out of the way, shall we?

Perhaps the most inefficient way of extracting stuff from your mind is to write it down sequentially so that someone else can understand. You force yourself to slow down and overthink things. Going step by step from what you currently do to paper (or word processor or a flow chart or anything written out) is painstakingly slow and fraught with missed steps. In short, don't do this. It doesn't work.

Now let's talk about the simple method that does work. The far better way to create a system for a process is to capture the process as you do it. The magic here is that you actually get the work done while creating the system for others to follow.

The idea of capturing systems is that you take your best-established processes and transfer the process in the simplest and easiest possible way to your team so they can do it properly going forward. How? Let me show you with a banana.

Chances are, you have eaten a few bananas in your life. Did you know that most people don't know the best way to peel a banana? Most people peel it from the stem, which means the banana often gets squashed, or is difficult to open. Too green and you can't open it easily. Too ripe and it gets mushed. But the solution to proper banana peeling has always been out there—monkeys do it. They hold it by the stem, pinch the opposite end, and the banana splits right open without a scratch.

How do you capture this process? It's already out there. On YouTube and a million other video hosting sites. Just go to You-Tube and type in "Best way to peel a banana" and you'll find the technique.

You can even use this as an exercise to get your team buying into the new way to create systems (by capturing the best practices by video, or using an established video that teaches the best practices you want to use). Here is the exercise: Buy a dozen bananas. Get a few employees you want to train with a system, to individually show you how they peel a banana. Don't have them do this together since they will try to copycat one another. And don't you dare stare them down and make them nervous. *Make no judgment.* Just observe. Some may do it the "right" way already. Likely, most won't.

Next, send them the video you find on YouTube on how to peel a banana. Have them watch the video and give them another banana to practice. Then have them meet with you again and show you how to peel a banana. Boom! System captured (thanks, YouTube) and transferred. The point here is, don't try to make it right or perfect before you get it off your plate. Just get it off your plate by capturing what you already do on video, or via a few other methods I am about to teach you. If you wait to establish the perfect process before you transfer it, you'll never find the time to get it right. So hand it off, then work with that person to get it right.

Now stop monkeying around with bananas and let's do this with what matters in your business.

SYSTEMS FOR STARTUPS

If your business is brand spanking new, you can easily argue you have no systems. I mean, you don't have anything, even in your head, to tell others to follow. What do you do then? Two things.

Remember that the transition from Doing to Designing is like a gauge or throttle, not a switch. You want to do the work for a period of time so you can learn and relate. Then you can capture what you learn to transfer it. Or you could take a shortcut and become a curator of other people's systems.

One search on YouTube will deliver dozens, if not hundreds, of systems for almost anything you need. Most of the work has been done for you. It may not be how you want it or the way you would do it, but the systems are there, and rated and reviewed by others. Want to have an invoicing process your team can follow? Search for "how to invoice customers." In the deck-building business? Search for "how to build a deck." Need your team to dig holes, pour concrete, and hammer in joists? Search for "how to dig a hole for a deck post," "how to pour concrete for deck footings," and "how to install deck joists."

The systems have already been created. Your job is to capture what is in your head, or to use what other people have already captured from their heads. Then you go about designing the process for your team to use the knowledge that is all captured, recorded, and ready to be rolled out.

CAPTURING SYSTEMS

Once you have identified what you need to systematize first, you next determine which primary process you are following. Are you 1) communicating (speaking or writing), 2) making a physical action (moving something), or 3) interacting with something (working on the PC, pushing keys on the cash register)? Or, of course, it can be a combo of all three.

If you or someone else in your organization is already doing the work, you (or that someone else) simply do the task and you capture it as you do it. Capture your system through recording devices. For example, let's start with work done on a computer, since that is so common. Let's say I invoice clients (which I have done) and my QBR is writing and speaking (which it is). I used computer-screen recording software to record my process. (I don't want to make a software recommendation here, as it is constantly changing, but I do have a list at Clockwork.life.)

As I perform the task, I just record the screen and narrate what I am doing. I then store the video in a directory labeled for that task. Now the person who is doing it has a training video they can use to replicate the process over and over again. Easy to find in the directory and easy to do since it is recorded, step by step.

Every company goes through a flow of steps in order to be sustainable. A company will do things to attract prospects, to convert those prospects into customers, to deliver products/services to those customers, and to collect and manage the cash throughout. This process is called Attract, Convert, Deliver, and Collect (ACDC), and the power of managing the ACDC of your business is about as epic as the band AC/DC. Just with less shouting and sweat.

How should you set up this directory structure of systems? Easy. Make it public and use the ACDC categories. I am going to dig deep into the ACDC flow of your business in the final step of applying Clockwork to your business, but for now I will go into the basics. Every company must consistently complete four major stages in order to keep itself in business. The business must:

1. **Attract**—Bring in new prospects interested in the company's offering.
2. **Convert**—Turn a portion of those prospects into customers.
3. **Deliver**—Supply the customers with the product or service as promised.
4. **Collect**—Ensure that the money promised by the customers is gathered.

The ACDC model has nothing to do with electricity, or the band, for that matter. But it is as important as electricity and as epic as Angus and Malcolm Young tearing out the opening guitar lick to "For Those About to Rock (We Salute You)."

Everything you are doing in your business will fall into one of these four categories. So on a sharing platform that your team can access, like a cloud-based drive, create a directory called SYSTEMS. Under that directory, create four more: ATTRACT, CONVERT, DELIVER, COLLECT. When you capture a market-

SAMPLE SYSTEM DIRECTORY STRUCTURE

SYSTEMS

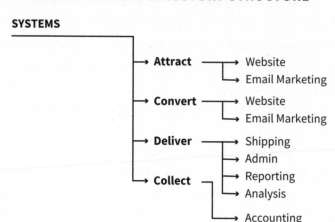

ing process, put it under ATTRACT. When you capture a process of shipping your product, put that under DELIVER. If you have a generic admin task that services all parts of the business, like cleaning the bathroom, put that under an ADMIN folder of DELIVER. Put all money-related systems, like receiving deposits, doing the accounting, and paying bills, under COLLECT. If you wish, you can change the name from COLLECT to CASH. The goal is to make it simple for you and your team to find the recorded systems when they need to refer to them.

Will the video capture address every anomaly? Not likely. But because it is much more of a show-and-tell, it conveys a lot more than you can with a written script. Plus, you just did the work while creating the training, so there is no time lost in building the system. Boom. Bam. Slam.

For other activities where you are talking (a type of communication process), all you need is a voice recorder. You probably already have one in your pocket: your smartphone. And for the physical stuff you just need a video recorder, which you already likely have, too. That same smartphone.

Capture the activity, store it in a folder system that is accessible to your team, and then delegate it to another employee, virtual assistant, anyone. (Well, not *anyone*. The Starbucks barista is already too busy making your Ecuadorian medium roast coffee to take on your other tasks.) Just get it off your plate. Protect the QBR at all costs! (Okay, maybe not at *all* costs. But it is right up there with your child's life and properly prepared Ecuadorian coffee.)

In the beginning, employees may come back with basic questions that you forgot to include in the captured content you made. Maybe you made a video on how to ship stuff using the computer but didn't include the login. This is where you give them the answer, and now request that *they* make the next, new and improved, video. That is right. They start working on improving the system right away, and by recording they become the teacher. And we all know the best student is always the teacher.

Doing this has had a massive impact on my business. I noticed that admin tasks were clearly time consuming, and doing things like shipping books (which I did myself for years) and invoicing took me far from my QBR. I wrote the original SOP for shipping books, which quickly became irrelevant and was ignored. So I had to teach the person myself, which was time consuming and never retained. So I would teach again. Then, when a new intern replaced the old one, all the knowledge went out the door and I had to train again.

I then went to the capture process I outlined above, and it was like magic. I just used a screen and video recording software package to capture the process on the PC of how to take an order and get it ready to ship. I took out my handy iPhone and filmed myself packing an order and explaining details on how to pack. That video and PC recording were all it took. I haven't shipped a book since. The team does it. When the next person starts the process, they review the video. Amazon changes its shipping process pretty regularly, so when the process needs to be updated, whoever is currently doing the process records a new video. And since the person making the new video (teaching) is the best student, they both reinforce the process in their own mind and have a training video ready for the next person.

We did the same for invoicing and paying bills. Video done. Recording done. The work gets done to the standard. And invoices go out.

Once the systems are delegated, figure out your measurable for it and to whom it needs to be reported. For example, I want to know that invoices are going out and money is coming in. The metric is simple: what new projects have come in and what do the accounts receivable look like. After a five-minute review, I know whether the system is humming along or if there is an issue that needs to be resolved. I'm not trying to seem too manic about efficiency, but I do want to drive the point home: I have the report taped to the left of my computer monitor once a week. When I come back to the office from speaking tours, I see the report instantly (without even needing to turn my computer on). If I have been away for three weeks, then there are three new reports. Simple. Fast.

The key is to always have one person accountable to the outcome. Make that point abundantly clear. That way, you know who to talk to when there are problems in need of a solution. On the wall in my home office, I have a quote from one of my heroes, George Washington, in which he addresses the importance of singular accountability. "My observation is that whenever one person is found adequate to the discharge of a duty, it is worse executed by two persons, and scarcely done at all if three or more are employed therein." If a founding father of the free world felt this was of critical importance, you and I should consider the same.

As you move into the Designing phase, always look to simplify processes to get the same (or better) results than in the past, with less effort.

While on a speaking tour in Australia, I had dinner with Craig Minter at the Potting Shed in Sydney. Craig is an efficiency consultant who goes into businesses and looks for obvious opportunities for the business owner to create organizational efficiency. After chatting over a beer about everything from tinnitus to long distance running to optimal footwear, Craig explained how he works.

"You often can make the biggest strides in streamlining a business through effective delegation. That's why the first thing I look for is where the owner may not be delegating decisions. Then, I determine the decisions they must make for their business to run like clockwork, and where those decisions are distractions," Craig explained.

According to Craig, the owner is usually doing something with the QBR (though he doesn't use this term) or other important tasks, and then they get distracted with decisions that take them off their game. If decisions are being pushed up the organization, distractions are happening and time piles (idle or waiting time) appear. And if a time pile appears, Craig looks to change the process so that decisions happen faster and with less distraction. He usually can.

Craig went on to tell me what he calls his "traffic light" story, about Debbie Stokes and her curtain manufacturing company, R&D Curtains. "Debbie was spending two hours a day making decisions. Every time a job was done, the leader of the work crew would come knock on Debbie's door and ask what they should do next. She would stop what she was doing, go to the floor, and evaluate the work. It only took her a few minutes to figure out what the next job was, but then another fifteen minutes or so to get back to the project she had been working on before the interruption. Then, the next knock would come."

Debbie hired Craig, who implemented a system where they put a red, yellow, or green tag on each job order. Now, with this "traffic light" system, Debbie's crew knows which job to work on next, and they don't knock on her door to ask her for guidance. She spends about ten minutes a day sorting all of the jobs for the next day, adding red, yellow, or green tags. Red signifies something urgent and needs to be done next, green is a project that still has adequate time before it is due, and yellow is in between. The team knows the simple rule: make decisions throughout the production day that keep work in the green or back to green as soon as possible. Debbie can now spend more time making big-picture decisions and strategizing next steps for her company.

While you may not be able to reasonably capture every task and delegate it, with a simple solution like Craig's "traffic light" system, you can find ways to trim down the work for the individual serving the QBR and transfer the rest out to the team.

FREEDOM LEADS TO MASTERY (OR THE 30,000-FOOT VIEW)

Earlier in the book I shared my friend Scott Oldford's insights about the delegation mind-set. Scott sells educational products, and using his delegation process, he has freed himself from doing any task in his business, including the QBR. He now spends his time looking at his company from the 30,000-foot view, which allowed him to achieve something most entrepreneurs never do: mastery.

Scott and I met at a Mastermind Intensive where I picked his brain, and he was so kind as to reveal exactly how he freed himself from the QBR. This is what I learned:

1. Scott first explained the mind-set of delegation, which is worth going over again. He explained that every entrepreneur and business leader knows they need to delegate, just like you know you need to do it. But the mistake is that most people believe delegation is a 10 percent you/80 percent them/10 percent you quotient. You devise what your team needs to do and task it to them (that's the first 10 percent). Then, they do 80 percent of the work, and the remaining 10 percent is still you making decisions and measuring results. Scott explained how this is just a trap. Either you have none of it or you have all of it. We need to get to none.

2. The process of delegating is not a magical switch of handing something off to someone else and everything is roses. Instead, Scott explained, you go through stages. The first stage is giving tasks (but you still make decisions). The second stage is giving responsibility to make decisions (but they don't own the result they are trying to achieve). The third stage is allowing determination of the result of tasks (but they don't own the outcome, which is the benefit it will deliver to the company). And the fourth stage is getting employees to own the outcome. This is a process of education in which you must give the tasks and responsibilities first, but then grow and guide the employee to knowing how they want to impact the company and working back from that.

3. When your employees don't execute the task the way you want, you will, like most entrepreneurs, probably get upset and accuse the employee of falling short. But the real reason you're dissatisfied is because you didn't give enough detail or guidance when delegating (which is why entrepreneurs tend to revert to the Deciding phase). Most entrepreneurs, in their head, know exactly what they want, but they don't put it into words (um, or let's see, a video recording). Scott's example is that we see the perfect oven in our head. It has six hundred parts. Yet all we tell the employee is, "Give me something that cooks food." The employee comes back with a pile of sticks and two rocks to rub together. Then we get upset that "they can't do what I want," but that's because we haven't told them what we want.

4. Scott's fix to this problem is to have his employees interview him (with a recorder at their side so they don't miss a single detail). This is a way to get freedom from the

tasks. You can capture what you do for highly replicable tasks, but some things are more nebulous. Having someone interview you brings out the details. People can't read what is in your mind, but they can get it on paper. They can proactively ask you the questions that they have or believe they will have. They can ask all the questions necessary to take your vision and make it into something doable. And by asking these questions, they alleviate that second 10 percent where they are coming back to you with questions after the fact. You are a visionary, but you may not communicate it well. So, let them interview you. Let them document it. Let them get your input the first go around, not via a back-and-forth.

This interview process has allowed others to carry the QBR and still adhere to Scott's vision.

Before we wrapped up our conversation, Scott said, "Focus has compound interest, Mike. Entrepreneurs try to serve everyone and do everything. They never master anything. My company is running on its own, and I devote my time to just knowing the market. I know my customers so well that I can move a million times faster than my competition. Not working in my business has given me the freedom to make moves so fast that my competition is blurry eyed."

RIVERS FOLLOW THE EASIEST PATH

As you give your workers tasks, especially the responsibility for making decisions, some may still keep coming back to you for your input—even if you have captured the systems you want them to follow. From their perspective, it makes sense, because what if

they make the "wrong" decision? They are concerned about being reprimanded by the boss (you), or worse, fired. They surely
don't want to lose your trust. But if you make the decisions for
them, they can do no wrong. If you give them an answer and it
works, they are rewarded for following your instructions. If you
give them an answer and it doesn't work, it's not their fault. Either outcome, as long as *you* make the decision, is safe for them.
And bonus—they don't have to think! They just have to do. (And
you already know that "doing" is your preference, so why wouldn't
it be theirs, too?)

The natural tendency of people is to defer decisions. We do it
at work and at home. Ever catch yourself saying "yes, dear" to
your significant other's request? It's easier than arguing, right?
It's easier for your employees to do the same.

If you are meeting resistance from employees you've empowered to make decisions, whatever you do, don't make their decisions for them! You must let them do the research, determine the
course of action, and then commit to it. After all, we are trying to
get you out of the business, and you can't do that if you keep
making the decisions.

Your employees may resist this by coming to you for assistance
in decision making, but you should always push the decision making back to the employee. If they ask for direction, respond with
"What do you think we should do?" If their plight of avoiding a
decision continues with the popular "I don't know, that's why I
am coming to you" answer, respond with: "We hired you because
you are smart and driven. We hired you to find answers. Please
come back to me with your best answer and the decision you
would make, and we will discuss." When they do come back, get
ready to smile, nod, and give your okay.

Even as they offer up ideas that you disagree with, bite your
lip and support it. Then, after the decisions and actions have

been carried out, for anything with significant outcomes—either positive or negative—do a debrief and have the employee share what they have learned and what they will do differently the next time. Always do the debrief *after* they make and execute on a decision.

The only time to intervene is if you see them making a decision that will have extreme and dire consequences. If you spot severe danger, make your colleague immediately aware. Now you are mentoring them, not deciding for them.

In a must-see interview, billionaire Sara Blakely,* the founder of Spanx, explained the foundational belief that spawned her success: failure should be embraced. Blakely explained, "My dad growing up encouraged me and my brother to fail . . . It's really allowed me to be much freer in trying things and spreading my wings in life." The only way to make progress is by moving through challenges, mistakes, and errors, and learning on the way. This requires making your own decisions. Ultimately, as Blakely explained, the only true failure is idleness, where you don't make any decisions. Stop training your employees to be idle by deciding for them. Have them move your business forward by empowering them to make decisions.

How do you empower someone to make decisions? Brace yourself—you must reward mistakes. When something doesn't go right and you punish the person (lecture, point out what went wrong, chop their pay, anything), you instill fear of making the wrong decision, and therefore it is safest for them to just come back to you for decisions (keeping you in the Deciding phase).

---

* www.cnbc.com/2013/10/16/billionaire-sara-blakely-says-secret-to-success-is-failure.html

But if you say, "Hey, the outcome was not what we expected, but I am proud of you for making a decision to move us forward. I want you to keep at it and move us forward. Tell me, what can I do to serve you?," you will not only start to see your business run like clockwork, you will have improved your relationship with a member on your team.

Toyota's world-famous manufacturing process is based on the same core belief. The decision making must be pushed "down" to the people making them. When a line worker has a problem, he can stop the entire line (you read that right), while the managers hurry over to provide support for that person. The line worker gives out the commands and direction and the managers provide the support to get the line up and running again. That is empowerment and giving decision making to the right people— the people closest to the problem.

⚙ CLOCKWORK IN ACTION

1. Capture a system now. Yes, you have hundreds of systems you will ultimately capture, but you won't capture any of them if you don't get started. Take the first step now— something small and easy, and something that you can take off your plate permanently. Capture that first system and see how it works for you. And then have the person to whom you assign the system make the next version of the recording.

2. Store your first captured system in a directory that is accessible by your entire team. Set up a simple directory with folders labeled ATTRACT (marketing), CONVERT (sales), DELIVER (operations), COLLECT (accounting). Then, make the necessary sub-directory below the

appropriate ACDC folder for the new system you captured. As you and your team move along with capturing
systems, store them in the new folder structure you created. You rock star, you . . . we saaaaluuuute you. (That's
a shout-out to AC/DC the band, if you missed that.)

CHAPTER SIX

STEP FIVE: BALANCE THE TEAM

Nicole Wipp is an attorney who runs her own firm in Milford, Michigan, about forty-five minutes outside of Detroit. Before she designed her business to run automatically, her firm was focused on litigation, which she found overwhelming in terms of her time and the emotion involved in dealing with her clients' cases. Then Nicole had a baby and took a four-week maternity leave (sounds like the "four-week vacation" test for the business, doesn't it?). During that break, she decided she needed to make a permanent change.

When I was picking Nicole's brain about this book, she said, "I had to be brutally honest with myself, Mike. I had to think not only about what I should be doing, but what I should *not* be doing. Maybe I was capable of something, but was I really suited for it?"

Nicole analyzed her work habits and discovered that she was not good at traditional lawyer work, such as writing briefs. She was great with ideas, but not seeing them through. When she was fundamentally truthful about her strengths and weaknesses (and you need to be, too), Nicole realized, "I'm better at the first 20 percent of an idea, and the last 5 percent, but I am not good at everything in between. I needed people to handle the other 75 percent."

As she evaluated her workload, she monitored the energy involved in each task. "Tasks that drained me, even when I was just thinking about them, those tasks were not playing to my strengths. They caused me to procrastinate, and dredged up negative feelings that impacted me, and my team."

For some of you, daily work may feel like it's slowly chipping away at your soul. That experience must be transformed in order for you to not only love your business, but to grow it to its full potential. To do that, you must give the tasks that drain your energy to someone else. With those tasks off your plate, you can operate in the zone of flow—your own zone of genius.

Considering her own zone of genius, Nicole decided to transition her firm out of litigation and became the Family & Aging Law Center, the changed name showing the new intent of the firm. She not only got rid of the tasks that drained her; she eliminated the traditional lawyer offerings that she was not great at delivering. After hiring and restructuring staff, Nicole went from working one-hundred-hour weeks, thirty days a month, to working just *five days a month*. And she did it without dropping her annual income. Many entrepreneurs fear their personal income will drop off when they hire someone, so I pressed Nicole to explain that point further.*

"For a brief period after I started this process, my income did

---

* If you are familiar with the Profit First method, there is a powerful, simple add-on you can use to make sure your business is ready for that next hire. Set up a bank account that is called "Future Employee." Then start allocating a percentage of your company's income to that account, representative of the salary that you believe you will be paying. This will prove your company can afford the employee *before* you hire them. And when you do make the hire, you already have a cash reserve for their salary. Nice!

drop a bit. But it went back up as soon as I found the right team and they came up to speed," she said. "Even though there was an initial drop, on an annual basis, I made more." The lesson there is, when you consider hiring, look at the annual impact, not just what might happen in the next few weeks.

Nicole's firm is now more profitable than ever. She accomplished this by hiring the right people to do the right things, which freed up her energy so that she could maximize what she does best. Then she had to balance that team so that *they* also did what they do best.

"I didn't start off with a good team," Nicole told me. "There was a ninety-day run when I cried every day because my team was so bad. But what I realized was, it was me, not them. I had to reset and restart, and make sure I was hiring people based on their zone of genius, which complemented my zone of genius." (That's a lot of geniuses!)

Nicole works just five days a month and she's more successful than ever. She doesn't do any QBR work, which for the firm is spot-on legal work. She focuses on managing the business flow. Do you see how replacing yourself—especially in terms of the work you do that does not feed your soul—can only help your business to grow?

From the moment you make your first hire, part-time or full-time, or bring on your first virtual assistant or contractor, your company has multiple gears and you need them to mesh harmoniously. If you build a balanced company from the get-go, you will have a stronger foundation and it will be easier and smoother building from that point. Master the skill of balancing your team, starting with your first employee. This is a Designing skill and mastering it early will carry you far.

As Verne Harnish says in *Mastering the Rockefeller Habits*, we need to get the right people, doing the right things, right. This is true. Very true. But there is one additional element. The right people need to be doing the right things in the right amount. My modified version of that maxim reads like this: *Have the right people, do the right things, in the right portions, right.*

Here's how that sentence breaks down:

1. "Have the right people . . ." This means that you know the super strengths of your team, that you know their zones of genius. Not what they do most, currently, but what they are best at doing and get the most joy from. When a person is great at something and loves doing it, they will excel. Unfortunately, most business owners and leaders don't know the strengths of their people. Determine your people's strengths (and evaluate the strengths of people before you bring them on) and use this knowledge to put them in a position where they will excel.

2. " . . . do the right things . . ." Identify what your business needs and what it doesn't. *Trash* what it doesn't need so that no one is distracted by these tasks. *Transfer* the work to the right people. *Trim* the work that can be made more efficient. When you do that, you are aligning the right people with the right things.

3. " . . . in the right portions . . ." People and your business both need balance. All the Doing in the world will fall short if there is no clear direction. And all the direction in the world is useless if no one is taking action on the strategy. Even if they are great at something, your team needs balance, and they need their own appropriate amount of variety.

4. " . . . right." This is about education. Provide your people with the relevant captured system. Have a clearly defined

outcome and process to follow. Educate them on what the QBR is and the necessity to serve and protect it.

THE RIGHT PEOPLE

Part of my book-writing process is testing and refining the book's core concepts and processes by actively sharing them from the stage, getting intrepid entrepreneurs to try them out on their business, and taking as much feedback and questions as I can get. If my audience can grasp the concepts and knows how to apply them to their business within sixty minutes or less, it is a solid process. If it is hard to explain or hard to grasp, or if the entrepreneurs aren't getting great results, the book isn't there yet and I need to head back to the drawing board.

I delivered my first big keynote on Clockwork to four hundred people at a conference in San Jose, California, on November 27, 2017. This was my tenth time presenting Clockwork; all the prior speeches were delivered to small audiences of twenty or fewer. On this occasion, everything clicked, for everyone. The metric of measurement is pretty simple. After the speech, do people come up to me in droves and talk about what they learned, the *ahas* they had, and the actions they plan to take? Or do they scurry out of the event as fast as possible, leaving that one weirdo with an indiscernible funky smell to tell me his life story and talk about the skin rashes that appear all over his body when he sits for too long? (Seriously, that is exactly what happened at my second Clockwork speech. The book wasn't *quite* there yet.)

After I finished the first home run speech on Clockwork, I stayed in the room for another forty-five minutes answering questions, listening to entrepreneurs' stories and what people were doing to streamline their businesses. One entrepreneur, Andrew

Berg, who was in the audience on my ninth attempt presenting Clockwork, was so inspired by it that he flew himself and his executive team from their New Jersey offices to the San Jose presentation to hear the tenth version. Andrew approached me, introduced me to his team, and then looked at them and said, "See. I'm not crazy. We have to declare, protect, and serve our QBR."

As the audience funneled out of the room, I noticed one gentleman waiting patiently for me. If you are a speaker, you will know this is usually the weirdo, and you should avoid eye contact at all costs. But this guy I recognized. It was Darren Virassamy, cofounder of 34 Strong.

Darren is *the* expert on balancing teams and bringing about extraordinary engagement from every employee. His company has taken the StrengthsFinder system, which measures an individual's talents (among other things), and developed a powerful process to move the right people into the right roles at a business.

Darren and I started chatting and decided to continue our conversation over dinner, where he proceeded to school me on balance. I realized then that, even though the QBR strategy worked, and resonated with audiences, a company would still have to balance its team in order to achieve organizational efficiency.

"The mistake organizations make, both big and small, is that they see all people as basically the same. If you can talk well at an interview you are hired. If you can kiss ass well once you're hired, you get a promotion. The work, of course, matters, but the measurement is simply whether you can do an adequate job in the time allotted," Darren said. "What's missing is the realization that every person has an extraordinary talent. The person who turns red-faced in an interview and can barely spit the words out may be the best analytical mind in the world. That person who talks about the importance of serving others may not be a good sales-person who is motivated by numbers, but may be a powerful customer service person who is motivated by impact."

He continued, "You need to know what people are inherently strong at, and then match them to the role in your business where they are applying that strength as much as possible." In other words, if you measure a fish by how well it can climb a tree and a monkey by how long it can breathe underwater, you have set up both for failure. But if you measure the fish by its ability to breathe underwater and the monkey by its ability to climb a tree, you will find they excel.

For your people, match their strength to the role. How do you find their super strength? You ask them. Well, it is a little bit more involved than that. For example, if you are interviewing someone to write content for your website and you say, "What is your strength?," if they have even a modicum of desire to land the job, they will likely say, "I'm really good at writing copy."

So the question is not what you are good at; the question is what do you naturally love to do. For example, "What are the three favorite things you have ever done at work?" "If you were able to have any job on the planet, doing anything you want, what would you do?" "Ten years from now, what is the perfect job you see yourself doing?" "If you had all the money in the world, and simply wanted to work for the joy of working, what would you do?" Seek out their interests. Seek out their hobbies. Seek what gives them joy. Because if it gives them joy, it is usually their strength.

That's the shortcut. For my own business I use a far more thorough approach. I did 34 Strong's team evaluation and took their direction in moving the right people into the right roles (which we'll discuss in a minute). As new hires are considered, we interview with the questions above and have Darren test them out for us.

As we said goodbye, Darren reached out to shake my hand. Me, not being the master of human cues, didn't even notice, subsequently invoking the most awkward hug of all hug moments. His outstretched arm was now pinned between our abdomens, as I clung to him for a weirdo length of time. We both cleared our throats, but nothing would overcome the pinnacle of awkwardly long, pinned-arm man-hugs.

Now that you are working toward a target 4D Mix, have identified your QBR, and are mobilizing your team to protect and serve the QBR, you'll notice that your team may need to shift to accommodate these changes. This is where you will sometimes get pushback from your staff. People may worry about their job security, or they may have a difficult time letting go of their old roles. Or you may find yourself locked in your own awkwardly long hug. As you go through this process, keep in mind that transition can be difficult for some people. In this chapter, I'll share how to balance your team, and also address some potential issues that may come up in the process.

WHEN SHOULD I HIRE?

I get this question almost daily. Before I can answer, the person asking already has their own answer. They'll say, "I can't afford to hire someone now," and "No one will have the skills I need, without a huge price tag," or "Everyone else sucks." The entrepreneur's conclusion is almost always the same: "I guess I just need to grind it out longer by myself." They decide they need to delay the hire, and in doing so, stay stuck longer and longer in the Survival Trap. A good rule of thumb is, if you feel you could use help but need to grind it out longer, take that as a desperate subconscious plea to yourself that you need help now, and should make that hire. Remember Celeste's story at the beginning of this book? No one wants Celeste in that position, working herself into exhaustion and illness, and we surely don't want it for ourselves. But if the mentality is to just grind it out for yet another day, you are slowly but surely digging yourself a hole that will become harder and harder to get out of.

First, let's address your mind-set about doing the work yourself. Let me ask you a question. Would you rather make fifty dollars an hour or five dollars an hour? Of course you want that fifty bucks. What if I asked you if you would rather make fifty dollars an hour doing all the work yourself, or five dollars an hour doing no work at all? This is where the Survival Trap reveals itself. Fifty dollars an hour is still better on an hourly return than five dollars an hour, but how much you ultimately earn is determined exclusively by your effort and your ability to sustain. The five dollars an hour (after expenses) comes in regardless of whether you are working or not.

When you figure out that you can keep multiplying five dollars an hour into infinity, you might change your thinking. Let's say with one good hire you can make five dollars an hour without working, and with two hires you can make ten dollars an hour. With ten hires you can now make fifty dollars an hour without lifting a finger. You're sick, you make money. You go to your daughter's school play, you make money. You go on vacation, you make more money. That is the goal of a Clockwork company— that the company runs itself without any dependency on you, all while serving you with the money it creates.

Now that you see you *can* make money even (or especially) if you don't do the work yourself, when should you hire? Hiring can't happen too soon. But it *can* happen too fast. Those are two different things. If you hire too fast, you are hiring flippantly and without proper consideration. That is a mistake. But you can't hire too soon. Meaning, any size business will benefit from the right hire, hired under the right parameters, sooner rather than later. For example, say you are in a routine of doing the work yourself, and that it is relatively consistent, but you are not making nearly enough money for yourself. It's time to hire. Don't be distracted by the immediate feeling of "I don't have money." Think long-term: "I need a way to make more money, without working more." This is a time to hire, under the right parameters. Meaning, maybe you aren't ready to hire someone full-time with benefits. Maybe you want someone to work five hours a week, and you can only realistically pay them ten dollars an hour.

Now you may be thinking, "Who wants to work for fifty dollars a week?" There is someone out there who would be thrilled to find a job like that. The mistake entrepreneurs make is to think that all people are seeking full-time jobs, and that all people expect top dollar. For example, Erin Moger has worked part-time for Profit First Professionals from day one. She doesn't want to work more; she wants to raise her young family. My business partner, Ron Saharyan, and I are both humbled to know her and to work with her. Erin is an amazing team member. So we created a position that is a big win for her because it respects her time, and she serves our company, caring for our members in extraordinary ways. That's a big win for us.

The first hire I brought on, Jackie Ledowski, worked three hours a day, three days a week. It was perfect for what she wanted in her life at the time and she was perfect for me. I was now able to transition the Doing to her—for nine hours a week, at first— which allowed me to Design more.

The goal for early stage hires (and every stage hires, for that matter) is to free you up to focus more on Designing and less on

Doing, and that can't happen soon enough. Remember, you need to make money without doing the work. Every dollar you make via your company's effort, and not your own, moves you closer and closer to becoming a Clockwork company.

WHOM SHOULD I HIRE?

The great irony is that you should not hire people based upon the skills on their résumé. The only thing you can give people is skills, and you want to give people the skills to do the work the way you do it. "Skill" jobs can be a trap. When you hire someone who has the skills already, it means they are walking in with the baggage of their past work. They will apply the skills you need, their way, which is rarely the way you want or need the job done. This means there will be, best case, confusion and inconsistency, and, worst case, the need to redo work.

You want to hire people with a great get-it-done attitude, high energy, and high intelligence, people who are a strong cultural fit and who have a desire to do the work you need done. All these are intangibles that can't be taught. Either they have it or they don't. So seek out people who have the intangibles you need, then give them the only thing that you really can: the skills.

Once you realize that you don't need a "senior specialist with ten years' experience in social media and product distribution," you could theoretically hire a teenager who has the right attitude, energy, intelligence, and fit to do the same work. Well, that's not theory; that is exactly what we did. My office has a teenager who runs our social media and handles product distribution. Since she's a minor, I'll change her name to Alice. She may be minor in age, but she is a majorly great employee. (See what I did there?) Alice works for a little above minimum wage—not because we are taking advantage of her, but because that was what she wants for her first job. Oh, and she can't work until after school gets out at three o'clock, wants time off for sports and band, and needs to be able to walk to work or get a ride from her grandpa, which are all things that we gladly accommodate.

Remember, people don't pick jobs based on just pay and vacation. And if that is the only consideration those people are making, you don't want those people, anyway. Yes, people want pay to live their lifestyle and vacation and to do other things, but good employees are also looking for something deeper. Fun, learning, impact, culture, and more.

When looking for new team members, seek diversity. The biggest mistake we make is hiring people whom we like. If we like them, it is usually because they are like us. We need people with different skills and points of view. Hire diversity. Don't hire people you like; hire people you respect.

Finally, be a trait-seeker. Look for employees with the traits and strengths you need. *How to Hire the Best* by Dr. Sabrina Starling details an excellent approach to, well, hiring the best. In your trait-seeking role you will want to determine whether this person needs to be super detail oriented, or a great communicator, or analytical. Consider the different jobs you need completed at your office and the specific traits those jobs need, and then hire for them.

Ever notice that when you run an ad for an open position, you get dozens or hundreds of applicants who are not really interested in the job? They are just applying to *any* job. Those people swamp your inbox with résumés, and if you try to interview them they respond with things like "What job is this again?" or "What is the pay and how much vacation do I get?" and "What do I need to do again?" I am not suggesting these are bad people, but they surely are a bad fit for your company. And a big waste of your valuable time.

To find better candidates, create an ad that defines your culture and disqualifies the résumé spammers all in one shot. How do you pull off that little miracle? Create a looooong ad that describes your culture in detail, prepares potential employees for the fun and not-necessarily-fun job requirements, and embeds a little requirement in the ad itself. For example, near the end of the ad, require that an applicant respond with "I'm pumped for this job" in the email subject line of their response. You will find that the vast, vast majority of applicants won't do this, which means they did not read the ad and are not truly interested in the job, or they are spamming, or they aren't able to follow instructions (a critical ability). On Clockwork.life, I share one of the best job ads I posted; you are welcome to copy, tweak, and paste it to attract your own part-time or full-time rock stars.

YOUR BIGGEST FEAR—TRUST

I need to get super real with you about something. Do me a favor, just peek around for a second and make sure no one else is listening in. We good? Good. Now get closer to the book. Closer. Lean in a little bit more. That's it . . . just a little closer. *SLAP!* There—I slapped you in the face with my faux-leather driving glove. Now that I have your attention, listen up! You have a fear issue. Better said, you likely have a trust issue. (Yes, making you lean into the book and then slapping you may have not been the smartest way to gain your trust, but I need to wake you up to this.) The most common reason that businesses fail to grow and run like clockwork is not the system. Shoot, there are a lot of wildly helpful scaling systems out there, like Gino Wickman's *Traction*, Michael E. Gerber's *The E-Myth*, and Verne Harnish's *Scaling Up*.

Yet most people who follow those systems, the Clockwork system, or cherry-pick from all of them, still fail to scale.

Why? Because they can't trust other people to run the business. I mean, imagine bringing on a key employee who walks in to help with the business and then walks out with all your clients months later. This can and does happen. Imagine that new employee you entrust to take care of clients screwing up and losing you a key client forever. The risk feels too great to trust others. I could tell you to "buck up" and get over it, since you need to trust your people so that you can successfully remove yourself from the day-to-day. But that's like telling you to just buck up and run a marathon when you've never trained for it. The risk of injury is too great, and therefore you may back down and never do it.

So, instead, we are going to do this slowly. Think about marriage. Chances are you don't just go up to a random person on the street and ask them to marry you. If you did that, you would probably get slapped again, with more than a faux-leather glove. You don't just get married. More likely, you go on a date or two, or two hundred. You probably spend time learning about each other. Maybe you move in together for a while before tying the knot. There is a courtship . . . usually.

But when it comes to key hires or even business partners, decisions are often made way too quickly. You know a potential business partner for twenty-four hours and feel that is adequate to enter into an agreement to run a business together for life. You will literally spend more time with this partner than your spouse, and yet spend so little time vetting him or her.

So move slowly with hires. Build the trust gradually. When you delegate, as Scott Oldford says, start with handing off the task, then the decision making, then responsibility for the result, and, finally, responsibility for the larger outcome to the company.

HOW DO I ALIGN MY TEAM?

The first step in aligning your team is understanding your (and, by extension, your business's) soul. What is your purpose? Your corporate mission? Purpose is the intersection of something that gives you joy and has a positive impact on others. For example, my life's purpose is to eradicate entrepreneurial poverty. Alone, it sounds like a tag line, but it means a lot to me. I made my business an amplification of my personal purpose. It is our corporate mission.

When I consider new members for my team, I talk about what our mission means, how I feel it impacts our world, and why it is important to me. They may or may not find it important. Some can relate; others can't. Those who can't, even if they are great employees, won't have a compelling mission pulling them forward. They may do well, but are not compelled to stay or do extraordinary things, since the mission does not speak to them.

If you have not defined your life and your business's purpose, don't worry; it can be done anytime. But until you do it, you won't have the ultimate tool for aligning employees within a company and an energizing force to pull the company forward. You can look to your QBR for clues about your mission.

Take Life is Good, for example. Its corporate mission is "to spread the power of optimism." I met the company's cofounder, Bert Jacobs, in Massachusetts years ago and he shared the story of how he and his brother John served their QBR. The brothers would host parties in their apartment where they had scrolled different drawings and phrases on the wall. In exchange for free beer, their guests would circle the drawings and sayings that they felt were most optimistic. That's how the marquee drawing of Jake and the company name, Life is Good, came to be. The QBR was the creation of optimistic phrases and drawings, and from day one Bert and John empowered the community to support the QBR. Genius.

When you have a corporate mission, speak about it often and in different ways, inside and outside the company. Tell new stories of when the mission succeeds and the impact it has. Share company folklore of what your company has done to deliver on the mission. Highlight and publicly award employees who deliver on the mission. The corporate mission is the reason you are doing what you are doing, and it is the wind in your sails.

The reason you need to be clear about your mission is to be sure you have the right people working for you before moving them into the right roles. The right people are a cultural fit. They do more than support the mission of the company (doing their job); they see themselves as an integral part of it.

Once you're sure that your team is in alignment with your mission, you can begin to move people into the right positions, and that begins with the Job Traits Analysis.

EXERCISE: JOB TRAITS ANALYSIS

Understand that a company position, such as a receptionist, salesperson, or something else, has a list of jobs/tasks required of that position. This list defines a round hole, yet people are square pegs. Finding someone who has traits that allow them to excel in every job/task that the position requires is unlikely. You are better served evaluating the strong traits your people have and matching those traits with the different jobs/tasks, regardless of position titles. For example, someone who has excellent phone skills may be great for some aspects of reception work, sales work, and customer service. At the same time, their disheveled presentation may make them unsuitable for other aspects

JOB TRAITS ANALYSIS

JOB/TASK	EXCEL TRAIT	IMPORTANCE QBR/HIGH/MEDIUM/LOW	CURRENT PERSON SERVING JOB	BEST PERSON SERVING JOB

FIGURE 17
(downloadable and printable versions available at Clockwork.life)

of reception work, sales work, and customer service work. Your goal: Match people's best traits to the jobs and tasks that need those traits.

In this next exercise, you will conduct a Job Traits Analysis.

1. In the left column, fill in all the jobs and tasks for a position in your company. Do this for all the positions you have in your company, including your own.

2. In the Excel Trait column, enter the primary behavior that would allow a person to excel at this job/task. For example, if a job/task is "Managing Inbound Calls from Customers," the Excel Trait may be "professional and confident voice" or "empathetic and clear communication." Don't get into minutiae like "ability to dial on keypad," or "can transfer calls." Yes, that stuff is necessary, but what we are looking for here is not the skills required (you can train on skills). We are looking for inherent

ability and enthusiasm that is difficult or impossible to train. Just write down one, not multiple, traits. What is the one critical trait that moves that task forward the most successfully?

3. Importance: This column is for the impact it will have on the company. Mark each task as one of these four levels: QBR, High, Medium, Low. QBR is the most critical level. High is the primary task that must be done when the QBR is protected. Medium and Low are necessary but not critical functions.

4. Current Person Serving Job: List any people who currently do this job or task.

5. Then fill in Best Person Serving Job by listing the person (or people) who, based upon the match-up with the trait, is best to do this work.

6. Then move people to the most critical tasks, starting with the most important first—the QBR. Match the person with a strength trait to the job that needs that trait. Move and observe.

7. People are *not* their titles. People are their strongest trait. You no longer are seeking a receptionist, for example. You are seeking "The Great Communicator," so identify who that person is and match them with the tasks and jobs that need a great communicator.

8. As such, we get rid of the traditional pyramid structure of organization charts, which focus on seniority and power/position. People need to "climb the ladder" and often move into positions that don't use much of their traits or abilities. A Clockwork company is not about the old pyramid structure; instead, it uses a web of connections, matching strength where strength is needed, resulting in a network structured like a brain.

USING INSIGHTS GAINED FROM ANALYSIS

Recall Cyndi Thomason's story about how she was able to free up her Doing time and grow her business when she discovered her company's QBR: providing peace of mind to her bookkeeping clients. As her team adjusted to the Clockwork approach, Cyndi realized she needed to make a few changes.

Bree, one of her bookkeepers, was having challenges. Though she was super friendly and the clients loved her, she was not performing at a consistent level. She was great at documenting her processes and was enthusiastic about helping her team members, but she was more of a big-picture thinker; details were not her strong suit. As a result, some of the clients who loved her became frustrated when she could not deliver the services in a consistent manner.

At this juncture, most entrepreneurs would conclude that the employee can't do the work they are supposed to, and fire them. But Cyndi is cut from the Clockwork cloth, as it were, and instinctively knows she must match a person's traits to the tasks that benefit most from those traits. She knew she had someone with an amazing natural talent for communication on her hands, and Bree would thrive if Cyndi had the work for her. The goal was not to *make* the work, only to find the work if the business could truly benefit from it.

At the same time, Cyndi's assistant, Sarah, was leaving to travel the world with her husband and agreed to help Cyndi find her replacement. In the process, Sarah told Cyndi about the challenges she experienced with her position. She said that having an accounting background would have made her better able to assist and take care of the load Cyndi was carrying.

As Cyndi and I worked to balance her team, making note of the tasks each team member considered to be joyful and their natural traits, it became obvious that the duties Cyndi needed to shed were actually related to Bree's skill set with setting up systems, creating education programs, and managing the marketing technology.

"The results have been amazing," Cyndi told me. "Bree is a dynamo. At first she was doing behind-the-scenes quote prep, and I talked to the client. She did so well with that, now she is screening the clients, prepping the quotes, *and* presenting them to the clients."

Moving Bree into a new position as Cyndi's assistant solved three team issues: it removed Bree from work that didn't suit her and into a position that she enjoyed, while also harnessing her skills and inclinations to tackle the unique challenges of the assistant's position, which allowed Cyndi to unload more Doing. When we understand what is working for our team members and what they are naturally inclined to do, we can move the right people into the right positions.

A few months later, right before this book went to print, Cyndi emailed me to say that for the first time ever, her company had engaged and begun to service a new client without Cyndi having any idea who the client was. Meaning Bree and the rest of the team were handling everything. Cyndi dropped a quick email to the new client and said, "I want to thank you for working with us." And the response came back a moment later, "I love your company. This has already been a wonderful experience. Thank you for all you and your team does." In the past, Cyndi was on the front lines of all communication with their clients. Now, a few short months after balancing her team, all she had to do was send one thank-you email to a very pleased client. That is Clockwork, my friend! Boom! Now let's do this for *your* business.

EXERCISE: CLOCKWORK TEAM TIME ANALYSIS

For a business to stay afloat and grow, it must be actively Doing things that its clients value. The Designing work is about creating the best way to do things your clients value, and have your company do those things on automatic.

Kyle Keegan owns a disaster (fire and flood) clean-up service, Team K Services, and he loves getting out there and helping people. He loves doing the work. He gets his hands dirty, literally, every week for at least a few hours. And he learns from the field how to make his company run better. The QBR he identified for his company is extremely fast and accurate estimates. This gives customers, who just hours ago in many cases experienced a disaster, a very quick understanding of how they can recover and what it will cost.

But Kyle realized that his Doing was stalling company growth. So he looked at his internal team to determine people's strongest traits and see whether anyone had the traits to serve the QBR. Once he figured that out, he could shift to more Design time and take his company to the next level. He found two ideal people for the role, and then balanced the team to ensure the QBR was protected and served, that the work was getting done, and that he had Design time to himself. To keep the business in balance he did the Team Time Analysis. You can, too.

Here's how you conduct your own Clockwork Team Time Analysis:

1. As I shared previously, the optimal percentages of work balance for companies is 80/2/8/10. Eighty percent is Doing: getting tasks done that directly or ultimately serve the customer and bring value to them. Two percent is Deciding for others: making necessary approvals, helping employees with decision making in unusual circum-

stances. Eight percent is Delegating the management of resources. To reiterate, Delegating is NOT making decisions for others; it means assigning ownership to others and providing the necessary leadership to bring about a larger outcome. Ten percent is Designing strategy. This is about making the other three levels—Doing, Deciding, and Delegating—more and more effective.

2. A single-employee company (just the owner) is the entire company. So their job/task breakdown should target 80/2/8/10.

3. When you have multiple employees, you want to balance the team to bring the average to 80/2/8/10. For example, your individual time may be 60 percent Doing, 4 percent Deciding, 16 percent Delegating, and 20 percent Designing. Assuming you have one other employee who works the same amount as you do, they will need to be 100 percent Doing in order to bring the aggregate of Doing for your company to 80 percent, as their 100 percent and your 60 percent averages out to 80 percent. Similarly, Deciding would now be 2 percent for the company (the average of you both), 8 percent for Delegating, and 10 percent for Designing.

4. Use the Team 4D Time Analysis chart to figure out the balance for your company. Put in each person. Weigh the amount of time they work for the company in relation to the total company. For example, if you work eighty hours a week (we need to fix that fast, by the way, because your working that much is not in the spirit of Clockwork) and another employee works eight hours a week, your work is weighted ten times more than the employee.

PUTTING IT ALL TOGETHER:
THE FIRST FIVE STEPS IN ACTION

Now that you've learned the first five steps to clockwork your business, I'll show you how those steps work together to not only streamline your business, but create massive growth. In this fictional scenario, we'll talk about Outlandish Dish, a culinary tourism company specializing in European excursions for English-speaking foodies primarily from Australia, Canada, the United Kingdom, and the United States. On their three-day "quick study" trips and fourteen-day "immersion" adventures, guests experience authentic local cuisine in different countries. They meet the chefs, learn the history of the food, and meet local farmers and artisans who create specialty items.

The owner, Roberto Nolletto, is an Italian expat who moved to Paris, where Outlandish Dish is headquartered. He oversees the company, runs its marquee trip four times a year, and develops new programs. Roberto started the business because he loved experiencing different food and cultures so much that he was doing his own trips and bringing friends. Eating a meal with Roberto and listening to the stories and history had his friends lining up to go with him, so he decided to launch Outlandish Dish and make a business out of his passion.

A common trip starts with dining in Geneva on the fabled cheese dishes, traveling through Germany to try their wursts (which, ironically, are their bests), enjoying the most incredible breads and pastas from Italy, and finishing the trip in France to feast on wine, pastries, and world-class entrées. The final night of each trip includes a cooking experience, where, under the guidance of a world-renowned chef, guests prepare a meal, dine, and then party the night away. These events have landed Outlandish Dish rave reviews and international press.

The problem is, even though the United States and Canada are the company's biggest market, they struggle to pull customers from there. They do heavy marketing in the US, yet only 20 percent of their customers are American; 80 percent of their customer base comes from Australia and the UK.

Roberto wants Outlandish Dish to run (and scale) like clockwork, but it is stuck. They generate $3.5 million in annual revenue, but the company is only marginally profitable. They employ twenty-five people, including Roberto, fourteen additional tour guides, one website developer, one marketer, two salespeople, three tour planners, one admin, and two bookkeepers. Roberto doesn't feel he can afford to make new hires, but at the same time his staff is maxed out. He needs more people to help market more effectively in the United States, and more tour guides. Roberto helps with the marketing, scouts new tours, and leads the marquee fourteen-day tours. He can't work any more hours, and he is exhausted.

As he begins the Clockwork steps, Roberto does the sticky note exercise for himself and his employees. Roberto is one of those "I can do everything" entrepreneurs, who fills a mix of roles at his company. He identifies his six crucial jobs as scouting out new tours, recruiting tour guides, connecting with his guests (and sharing stories), managing the cash, running the marquee tour, and maintaining relationships with vendors. Roberto has his team do the analysis, too, identifying the Primary Jobs for his peeps. For his tour guides, the Primary Job is the active management of a tour as it is in progress. The sales team's Primary Job is not to "sell to anybody" but to match the right trip to what people really want, as opposed to what they think they want. Everyone has a Primary Job, including Roberto, which is his almost uncanny ability to connect with guests. When he does, those guests become lifers, with more than half the guests coming back year after year, for a decade or more. If Roberto doesn't connect with the guests himself, the "repeat rate" of guests plummets to less than 20 percent.

With all the sticky notes of Primary Jobs on the table in front of him, Roberto goes through the deductive process until he is left with the "one for the wallet." It is clear what makes all the difference to the company, so Roberto declares his QBR is connecting with guests. He is such a good storyteller that people get excited about their adventure before the trip begins, stay excited while they are there, and talk excitedly about their trip after they get home.

Next, Roberto starts the QBR protection, which means that he has to first and foremost get rid of the task that is taking him furthest from the QBR: the marquee trip. He needs more time to connect with prospects and get them excited about taking one of their trips, and with guests who have booked upcoming trips. The tour guide assigned to take over does well, and Roberto's time is freed up in a big way. But soon after the first trip, complaints come in, and they all sound the same: "What happened to Roberto? Where are the stories?" Turns out, people loved the tour and the food, but they missed Roberto. As a result, his business is still stagnant.

At first, Roberto thinks he needs to go back to how he used to do things and do the marquee event by himself again, but he knows that is a fool's folly. It would just get him back to where he was before, to what wasn't working. He knows he needs to make his business run at a new level, and that requires that he think and *do* differently.

Because Roberto does *not* go back to running the big trip that took up so much of his time, he has time to think about his QBR. One night, while talking with his new in-house booker, Mariette, she says, "Our company QBR is storytelling. You serve the QBR.

Running an entire trip is not the QBR, but your story times are. Why don't we have you drop in on a trip near the beginning, and then again on the final night? Instead of running a trip for two weeks, you can serve the guests on the trip for a day or two. And, since almost all of our tours pass through Paris, our home base, many of these story times will have you out of the office for just four or five hours."

Roberto likes the idea but is skeptical. He knows storytelling is the QBR, but he struggles to believe that showing up only at the beginning and end of a trip will have a big impact.

Roberto is right. That small tweak to the approach doesn't have a big impact. It has a massive impact.

When he shows up for the mingling and dining parts of the trips, he is on fire. He isn't drained from travel, so he's able to be present in a big way. He regales the guests with stories, and they hang on every word. And, because Roberto isn't tied up for two weeks running the marquee adventures, he can now visit with every tour group, including those on the three-day trips.

Raves pour in. People who experience the three-day trip now start booking the fourteen-day trip. People want more adventures. They want more stories with their meals. And now, instead of 50 percent of just the marquee trip guests repeating trips, every trip is getting a 50 percent rebooking rate. Within a year, sales increase to $4.5 million. Outlandish Dish is no longer *one* of many culinary tourism companies; it is *the* culinary tourism company. It increases prices, and margins. Roberto captures systems for some of the other tasks on his six sticky notes so that his team can take over more of the Doing and give him more time for Designing.

Two problems remain: The first is that the team is still only twenty-five people, but with everyone focused on protecting the QBR, the demand has taxed the tour guide team and they need to make a new hire. The other is that sales from the US market continue to be a dribble.

Roberto does the Team Time Analysis to first address the challenge of his overloaded team. He evaluates the Team Time Analysis and discovers that this company is heavy in the Deciding, Delegating, and Designing phases, almost 40 percent. He is shocked, because his tour guides are constantly saying how busy they are (Doing).

Looking into it further, the percentages start to make sense. Roberto realizes his three tour planners are contributing to the skewed 4D Mix. Tour planners carry out many administrative tasks, and their jobs are heavy on Deciding (making decisions for tour guides), Delegating (assigning resources and responsibility to tour guides), and Designing (formulating a variety of new tours). As a result, these tour planners are also overloaded and stressed. Since most of the tours are already established, having three tour planners seems to be too many, as there's no need to create so many new itineraries. Instead of creating new tours, he decides to do more of what was working. He decides to keep the most successful existing tour and freshen it up every year with new restaurants and new chefs, but the rest can stay the same: same cities, same sites, same hotels, same transportation. This change frees up his tour planners and reduces all of the associated Deciding, Delegating, and Designing.

With the goal of supporting the tour guides who also need relief, Roberto does the Job Traits Analysis for his team. The key job trait for a tour guide is customer care. Roberto loves the tag line: "No one cares about how much you know, until they know how much you care." Knowledge of the area is important, addressing the problems that spring up as things move along is important, but nothing is as important as caring for the customer.

Evaluating the results of the Job Traits Analysis, Roberto notices that Janet, one of his three tour planners, is extraordinary at customer care. An American expat who moved to Paris to care for her grandmother in her final days, Janet fell in love with the city and all of Europe. In her work as a planner, her care for people shines. For example, she is known for sending gifts to the chefs and vendors she meets while scouting for tours, and staying in touch with them even if they don't become part of a trip. While she's never run a tour, she has the key trait that positions her for great success.

Roberto schedules a tour for Janet, and as tempted as he is to ride shotgun with her in this process, he knows the company must be designed to run itself. So he sends her to shadow an existing guide on one of the three-day tours. She learns from the guide, and on the third day she runs the trip. The other guides give Janet high praise. Then Roberto schedules Janet's first solo trip, and has the other guides pop in throughout the trip to give her support, which she rarely needs. On her second solo trip, Janet is completely on her own. Within a few months, she becomes one of their highest-rated guides.

Outlandish Dish still has a twenty-five-person team, and with a focus on improving successful tours rather than creating new ones, Roberto realizes that two scouts is too many. He looks at their traits. One of the scouts, Sankara, is a videographer and editor. Every time he gets a chance to make a video, he does. Roberto remembers a suggestion Mariette made at one point. She thought videos would be helpful to break into the US market, but Roberto couldn't fathom assigning that task to someone when most of his team was working overtime to meet demand. He asks Janet about this idea, and she tells him that Americans watch more video on Facebook and YouTube than they watch television.

Roberto matches the new job of tour videographer to Sankara's talent. Within two days, Sankara films the first video with

Roberto and Janet. Targeted for the US market, the video features Janet talking about the life-changing experiences Outlandish Dish provides. Then she introduces Roberto, who shares an amazing story of how Christopher Columbus crossed the ocean to discover the riches of America, and now he is personally inviting Americans to come to Europe to discover the rich foods. He shares stories of laughter and tears with his past American guests and invites the new guests to visit so that he can personally pour their wine on arrival.

The videos crush it on Facebook. Roberto is a massive hit; his charisma and charm are unmatched. Soon, Outlandish Dish has a rush of American tourists booking trips. Because everyone is in their right job, doing the right things, in the right portions, right, and because the entire team is serving the QBR, and because Roberto has enough time to focus on Designing his company, Outlandish Dish grows by leaps and bounds.

Americans start talking about the company, and then the unexpected magic happens: a major US network contacts Roberto about doing a show on European culinary tours. His natural storytelling ability serves him well, and once the show airs, he becomes a celebrity. Demand for his business skyrockets—well past $10 million in annual revenue.

You may think this is where the story ends, but Roberto is not done yet. His final step is to remove himself from the QBR. And wouldn't you know it? Janet shares the same trait Roberto is known for. She becomes the lead storyteller, especially for tours for Americans. Roberto enjoys his new career in television, and his team runs Outlandish Dish like clockwork.

The ending to this story may seem like a fairy tale, but any dream you have for your business, any goal you hope to achieve with your company, any contribution you hope to make to the world is possible when you are not hampered by work you shouldn't be doing, and when your team is running like clockwork.

Change is hard. I'm sure you don't need me to tell you that, but I'm bringing it up because, after implementing the first five Clockwork steps, you will surely be feeling it. Even when business is booming, and even when you have more time to focus on Designing your business, change can be stressful—especially when you're changing the balance of your team. Your staff (or freelancers) will also feel that change, and they may feel insecure about their new positions, or worry that they may be eliminated entirely. For those people who will remain part of your team, give them reassurance. Listen to their concerns. Affirm their place on your team. Remember to take time to breathe during this process. Yes, change is hard. It is also going to get you what you want: a business that runs itself.

CLOCKWORK IN ACTION

1. Balancing your team is an ongoing process, and it can't be accomplished in thirty minutes, or even a day. The exercises in this chapter will help you get there. Plan to focus on one exercise each week, and then evaluate the data to ensure the right people are in the right roles, doing the right things, in the right portions, right.

2. Do an analysis to ensure your company is at approximately 80 percent Doing. Make a note that when your company's resources expand or contract, it stays near that optimal 80 percent Doing.

3. Run an evaluation of your team to identify their strongest talents and traits. Then run an evaluation of the ten most important daily tasks your business must complete. Now match up the best traits of your people with the tasks that need those traits most.

CHAPTER SEVEN

STEP SIX: KNOW WHO YOU'RE SERVING

"We didn't go into places that promised big wins. We went into places we felt called to go into."

When Lisé Kuecker, owner of five Anytime Fitness franchises, shared her story with me over the phone one day, she made a point to tell me she had never lived in the same state as any of her franchises. Considering her husband was active-duty military at the time, that was some feat; they had moved states several times.

Growing up in New Orleans, where indulgent food is a major part of the culture, Lisé had seen obesity rates skyrocket. This influenced her interest in fitness, and soon, helping people lose weight and transform their health became her deep-seated passion, and then her company's Big Beautiful Audacious Noble Goal. When she began opening gyms during her husband's deployments, she didn't look to the biggest cities or the areas with high-income residents. She didn't even look to the communities in her own area, or within driving distance. She set up in towns that needed her the most—small towns that, on paper, didn't seem to have the potential to support membership growth.

"When we bought a failing franchise in Minnesota, the bankers and other people thought we'd lost our minds," Lisé told me. "We bought it for $50,000, which was basically the cost of the equipment. The gym had been on the market for a year and a half, and it was in bad shape—treading water the entire time. It was a miracle they had 350 members; that was in part due to the fact that the owners were local and well-loved."

Despite the fact that no one thought she could make a go of it, or should even try, Lisé was drawn to the dying franchise in small-town Minnesota. The obesity rates were quite high in the area, and she knew she could make a difference. She also knew that people who were living with obesity and struggling to lose weight were the people she wanted to serve. First, she cared about them and wanted them to succeed. Second, if she could help them, she knew she would have a better chance of retaining them as members than she would the average customer who may not have the same challenges to overcome.

"I rolled up to the gym in the bitter cold of February, me from the Deep South in my rental car with four-wheel drive," Lisé said, laughing. "Right away we started renovation plans, and I started calling members."

Over the next month, Lisé called every single one of the 350 members herself. She sometimes stayed on the phone for an hour or more, talking to people, asking them their opinions about the gym and about the changes they'd like to see after it reopened. She listened to their stories, their health goals, and the intimate details about their lives they wanted to share. After each phone call, she wrote down the most significant snippets about their life and their aspirations on a spreadsheet so she wouldn't forget.

The turnaround at the gym came fast. In less than a year, that franchise transformed to rank in the top 5 percent of all Anytime Fitness franchises. Do you want to know the real kicker? After the initial first month on-site, Lisé works an average of five hours a week on her business. No, that's not a typo. Not fifty hours. *Five hours.* Five hours total for *all* five locations. Just to be sure you're getting this: She works five hours a week Designing her business, not Doing. In the next chapter, I'll share more about Lisé and how she was able to pull this off. In *this* chapter, I want to talk to you about the next step in the Clockwork system: Make the Commitment.

The Commitment refers to where you target that awesome QBR power. All the power in the world is useless if it is not focused. Set a piece of paper outside in the sun and it will sit there, unchanged. Take a magnifying glass and concentrate the sunlight onto the paper, and you'll start a fire. That is the power of focused energy. The Commitment concentrates the awesome energy of the QBR in a way that will ignite your business efficiency (and growth) like never before.

The Commitment is an extremely simple, yet powerful, declarative strategy that involves clarifying whom you serve and how you serve them. Notice I didn't say "identifying" whom you serve and how you serve them. I figure you already have an idea of who your peeps are and how you serve them. This step in the Clockwork process is about homing in on that group within your customer base who are your best customers. I refer to them as "Top Clients." You may call them "dream customers," or "bestest friends," or, you know, "just like Mikes." Whatever you call them, you know who I'm talking about.

Once you clarify who and how, you must *commit* to that group, which is why this crucial step is called Make the Commitment. If you skip this step, I'm sorry to say you'll never fully realize what it means to have a Clockwork business—your business will be hampered trying to serve a group that is too broad to market to, sell to, and support effectively, and you personally will be far from free. You see, Clockwork is more than just creating the engine of your company (getting the internal stuff right); it is also consistently adding the right fuel for your engine—your Top Clients.

I suggest you post a declaration right above your desk, and in front of each of your employees' and contractors' desks. Just fill in the blanks:

Our commitment is to serve [whom] by [how].

Yes, it really is that simple. At my company, Profit First Professionals, *our commitment is to serve accounting professionals by giving them an exclusive, powerful way to distinguish themselves from their competition.* So what about Lisé? I'm pretty sure you can figure out whom she is committed to serving. But what about her "how"?

At Lisé's gyms, the QBR was customer support. "It was vital that we engaged the customer to help them achieve the fitness goals they wanted," she explained to me. "If they felt supported, and if we provided them with the education they needed to stay the course, we could get customers to use the gym for at least ninety days. Most people use a gym for thirty days and then quit, so attrition rates are high. At our gyms, we were able to achieve 70 percent retention after ninety days, compared to the industry average of 40 percent."

I'll take a stab at her commitment declaration: *Lisé's Anytime Fitness is committed to serving obese and overweight people who have struggled in their efforts to lose weight by providing them with specific education and customer support to reach their goals.* Does that sound about right?

The goal here is to craft a simple, effective statement. We are not writing poetry or fancy tag lines. We are simply getting clear on whom and how. In this chapter, I'll help you craft your commitment and show you why this is such an important step in the Clockwork process.

"EVERYONE" IS NOT YOUR MARKET

Repeat after me.

"Who?"

"Who?"

Let's try that again. You want to sound more like an owl.

"Whoooo?"

"Whooooooo?"

Ask "how" less and ask "who" more. Who do I serve? This is the most important of all questions a business owner who is looking to streamline their business can ask. Yet we rarely ask it.

When I ask business owners what niche they serve, many respond by saying some variation of "my niche is everyone," which, between me and you, is an oxymoron. That's like saying there was a dry rain today. Or that guy sitting next to you is a skinny fat guy. Or that Thanksgiving is a day of fasting. None of those things make sense. They don't exist and they don't make sense.

For a business to run like clockwork, you must have consistent delivery of your offering. You need to have a predictable process that yields a predictable output, and to do that you must reduce variability. Your predictability grows exponentially when you do fewer things for the narrowest set of expectations. What if Lisé decided to focus on multiple types of clientele? What if she marketed to and tried to serve bodybuilders? Or triathletes? Or skinny guys on the beach who get sand kicked in their faces by even skinnier guys? Would she be able to connect to all of her customers in the same way? Would they respond to her choices in the same way? Would they all want the same things from the facility? Would they all need the same type of education and support? Answer: That's a solid "no" across the board.

If you offer three products to five types of customers who each need their own variation of that product, you are delivering fifteen products. Better said, you are offering fifteen product variations, and for each one to be remarkable, you must get all fifteen right. That is fifteen areas of potential problems.

Now, let's say you have three products for one type of customer, where each customer has more or less identical needs. Now you only need to get three things perfectly right. It is far easier to get three things right than fifteen, and far easier to fix problems when they do arise.

Fewer things for fewer people result in fewer variations, which means you can get really, really good at what you do. And with fewer variations, you need fewer resources to get the good results. Simply put: Do less and you achieve more. (Yeah, I would highlight that one on your Kindle.)

Traditional teachings tell us to first determine whom we are serving and to modify our offering to meet their need. The popular term today is "pivot," but that term will change. It used to be "inflection point." Before that it was "paradigm shift." And before that it was "Soooo, what the hell should we do now?" The point is, you need to sell what the customer wants, otherwise you won't have anything to sell. On the surface, this theory seems to make sense, but it ignores the most important element of a successful business . . . you.

I have seen wonderful businesses pivot into disdain and failure. The owners keep shifting their offering to match what the customer wants until the customer starts buying. But in the process, they neglect to consider what *they*, the owner themselves, want. They ignore what their heart calls out to do. And they ignore that crucial final yellow sticky note: that thing that fuels their business. *They ignore their QBR.* And while the business may be winning customers, it is losing the heart of the owner and the soul of the business. I have seen many businesses pivot into something that the owner loathes. Sure, it may make money, but at what cost?

Dreading going to work is no way to experience life. This is why it is absolutely critical for you to first determine what you want. What you intend to be known for. What your soul sings out to do. That is why we must first discover your QBR, serve and protect it, and balance your team around it *before* we find the community that wants it. Don't pivot to the customers' desires. Instead, align your desires with the customers who want it. Don't pivot; align. Always.

WHO IS YOUR WHOM?

Now that you know what the heart of your business is (the QBR) and have galvanized your team around protecting and serving the business (the optimal 4D Mix), you can determine who of your clients can benefit most from it.

If you have a brand-new business with no clients yet, you can go through a variant of this process I am about to outline. If you have an established business that is serving a mix of clients right now, you have a leg up on finding the right customers who align with your QBR.

In *The Pumpkin Plan,* I outlined a process for identifying and cloning the best customers. The main point is, once you know who your Top Clients/Customers are, the next step is to "clone" them by attracting other clients or customers who have the same qualities. I'll take you through an abbreviated version of that process in a few, but first, I have one disclaimer: There is no guarantee that any of your existing customers represent the ideal community for you to serve. I have worked with my own clients on this process and a few of them did not have a single ideal client that we wanted to clone. That being said, the majority *did* have a client they wanted to clone, and if you too have one, it represents a significant shortcut to growing in that community.

Since writing *The Pumpkin Plan,* I have discovered two more elements to the process that you must know. The first thing I found is that while a psychographic—your customers' lifestyles, personalities, aspirations, values, and interests—does represent a niche community, those communities are very hard to access because they don't typically have the ever-important congregation points. Congregation points are where a like-minded community meets on a recurring basis to network, and share knowledge. Congregation points exist for almost all commercial industries, a lot of vocation groups, many consumer groups, and some life transition groups, but very, very few mind-sets.

For example, if you want to sell to vineyard owners (a commercial industry), there are countless vineyard associations. A quick Google search identified more than twenty-five, and there are surely far more than that. If you want to sell a product to airplane pilots (a vocation), there is a pilots association, shockingly named the ALPA, the Air Line Pilots Association. If you want to sell to wine lovers (a consumer group), there are wine aficionado groups. If you want to sell to first-time moms (life transition) there are groups for that. But if you want to sell to first-time mom airplane pilots who feel it is beneficial to drink wine while flying airplanes, good luck finding that group. It could be a mind-set that exists. I mean, Lord help us if it does, but that mind-set may be out there. But they surely don't congregate in any established and therefore predictable way, and therefore it is extremely hard to access this community. If your customers' psychographic does not have a community, you'll have to build one yourself, which is a herculean job—especially when you are flying planes drunk.

The acid test for the *whom* of your commitment is whether they have established congregation points and you can achieve consistent access to them. For example, my client Gary said that his best client is a single mom running a bakery business who has achieved her first $1 million in revenue, is overwhelmed by the work volume, and is trying to raise a child by herself. And because she can't stand her own mom, she has no help.

Gary (who I call Big G) told me, "Give me a dozen of this client. My profit will skyrocket, and I only need to do one thing for them. I found my niche!"

I said, "Let me ask you something, Big G. What I just heard is that you are looking to get more clients who are 'single mom entrepreneurs who hate their moms.' Right?"

"Exactly. That is exactly it."

I then asked Gary to tell me where their congregation points are. "Where do these people consistently get together to learn from and share with one another, Gary? Where does the SMHMBC meet? You know, the Single Moms Hating Moms Business Club."

The answer: nowhere. There are no meetups. No conferences. No podcasts. No websites. No single congregation point. Yes, two single-mom mom-haters could meet at some office holiday party and become besties. But happenstance is not a congregation point. A congregation point is a consistent presence to learn and share, and it doesn't exist for this group. This means Gary is impeded— there's no group to access. He can and should ask his one Top Client where she hangs out with other like-minded people in similar circumstances, because maybe there is some underground group.

But there is a low chance those groups actually exist, because Gary's psychographics are too narrow to warrant a community.

With this new knowledge, Gary took a fresh swipe at identifying a community. He asked himself what distinct elements about his favorite customer were also something that people formed communities around. She owned a successful bakery. That was one piece. She was overwhelmed with work. That was a second piece. She was a single mom entrepreneur. That was another. She also hated her mom. There was yet another.

With the four pieces identified, Gary asked himself, what elements spoke to his interests the most? Big G really enjoyed the bakery business aspect, because he loved manufacturing and that is what this basically was. He also felt he could empathize and support the single mom entrepreneur better than most vendors, since he was raised by a single mom entrepreneur and is a single parent himself. The other elements were not areas where he had interest or could contribute.

With the two elements identified, he ran the big test. Were there congregation points? With the power of Google, the answer was easy to find. Gary searched "bakery associations." Simple enough, right? Sure enough, he found the American Bakers Association, the American Society of Baking, the Independent Bakers Association, and more. He found online forums. He found Facebook groups. All of this meant that this was an established community, and that they congregate. That is opportunity!

When he searched for "single mom entrepreneur association," he found nothing. When he searched for "single mom entrepreneur group," he found one meetup group with twelve members. There is no question this is an important group of entrepreneurs, but it is not an opportunity for Big G to serve. The congregation points are not established, so breaking into the community will be very hard.

Gary decided to go after bakeries. He spoke with his best client, who was already a member of one of the associations, to get some suggestions on how to get involved. With that, Gary was off to going where his best prospects congregated. And like a good yeasty bread, his business started to rise.

Other people identify niches too broadly. They want to work with "rich people" or "small businesses." Those are broad communities, and while they may have congregation points, the knowledge shared is general and their needs are all over the place.

You need to identify a community that meets repeatedly at one or more congregation points to address their specific needs and wants. This is an area where you see the same prospects, vendors, and influencers appearing over and over. It doesn't need to be a physical meetup. It could be a Facebook group. It could be subscribers to a podcast or magazine. Ideally, there is a combination of ways for them to connect and learn. When you see this repetition of gathering and learning for a specific community, it means that you can gain access to the community and build a reputation for being the provider of the specific solution they need.

So let's find your *whom*. What follows is a super-short and *complimentary* version of the method I detailed in *The Pumpkin Plan*. If you haven't read that book, the next exercise will be enough to get the clarity you need to Make the Commitment. If you've already "Pumpkin-Planned" your business for explosive growth, please do this exercise anyway. The congregation point qualifier will give you new insights about your Top Clients.

1. First, evaluate your existing customer list. Sort them by revenue from most to least. This is important because the people who spend most on your product or service, particularly if they repeat purchases, are demonstrating through their behavior that they value you the most.

Don't trust people's words; trust their wallets. In other words, people can say how much they love you until they are blue in the face, but it is the action of spending money with you, or *not* spending money with you, that points to their true feelings.

2. Next, evaluate for the crush or cringe factor for each customer on the list. In other words, do you love them (crush), hate them (cringe), or feel somewhere in between (you know, a crunge)? You will automatically provide great service to the customers you love the most because it comes naturally to you. Conversely, you will find yourself avoiding or delaying work for the customers you hate, and the people in between will get hit-or-miss service from you.

3. Then, document the community each customer is in (industry, vocation, consumer group, or transition point).

4. Finally, determine all the congregation points. These are all the places where they hang out together in an organized group.

CRUSH / CRINGE ANALYSIS

CUSTOMER	CRUSH/CRINGE	COMMUNITY	CONGREGATION POINTS

I need to make a critical point to you. It is your interest in the community and the fact they have congregation points that is the most important thing. This is more important than how much you love your current customers. Having a great customer to clone is extremely helpful, but you can access a community even without a single client in that community. Further, a crush or cringe client may *not* represent the nature of their community.

The same is true for the customers you love. Realize that they represent a shortcut to the industry and possibly other great prospects. (Good people hang out with other good people.) Also realize that you may have bad customers within a great community, and that your jack-wad of a client is just not representative of that community and may not be the best way in.

The first lesson is to judge the viability of a market based on its congregation points. If it has many of them, and the community is active in multiple, that is proof that they are sharing with one another through established channels. Channels that you can access. Channels that you can market through. Channels where you can easily get a reputation for excellence. If you can't identify any congregation points, or if the points you do locate are few, scattered, and unestablished, you are in for a long slog. It is hard to be discovered when the community can't even find itself.

The second lesson is to go narrow and build toward broad. Most business owners try to start with a broad community and narrow their way down, and it doesn't work. For example, you may say your niche is the wine industry. But that could include vineyards, wine stores, wine distributors, importers, and exporters. The list goes on and on. Within the wine industry there surely are congregation points, but the same people don't go to all of them. That is key to finding a narrow niche—where the same people go to the same congregation points.

When you serve a broad niche—which is another oxymoron, like "act natural," "unbiased opinion," or "Kim Jong Un's hairstyle"—you may have to deliver variations of your product or service. What vineyards need may be different than what wine stores do. But the biggest problem is that the broader you go, the more expensive—both in time and in money—it becomes to be in front of the same group. They don't cross talk to one another, either, which makes scouting new prospects difficult and referrals almost impossible. It is less likely that a vineyard will be sharing best practices with a wine store, because they are in dissimilar businesses. It is more likely that vineyards will share with other vineyards and wine stores will share with other wine stores.

The problem amplifies, in that if you try to narrow your niche, you will be abandoning some established customers. Say you decide that wine stores are your best opportunity after all. Now you will need to take more and more attention away from vineyards, distributors, etc., and, by default, decrease your offering quality for them. Most business owners decide to start with a broad niche (which, I want to remind you, is not really a niche) so they have diversity and can get more opportunities. The result is they are actually diluting the quality of their offering and they will incur more expense in both time and money trying to break into the market.

SAMPLE CRUSH / CRINGE ANALYSIS

CUSTOMER	CRUSH/CRINGE	COMMUNITY	CONGREGATION POINTS
Example Customer	Crush	Flooring Tile	The National Tile Association
ABC Company	Cringe	Vineyard Owner	Winetime Podcast Winecon
XYZ Inc	Crush	Long-Haul Trucking	Freight Carrier Association The Cargo Conference

Take a lesson from Brian Smith, the founder of UGG. Years back, I spent a day talking to him about the stratospheric success of UGG, which I documented in my book *Surge*. I asked him, of all the things he did, what was the most impactful on his business success? "It's the niche, Mike," he said instantly, with an Australian accent: *neesh*.

The achievement of UGG's household brand recognition is due to its first ten years of niche concentration. UGG sold to the surfing community. The product was mastered for surfers—the material, the height of the boot, and the overall design were all created with surfers' needs in mind. Specifically, needing warm, dry feet. (The ocean is frigid in winter.)

By targeting a narrow niche, you master the next part of the Commitment. When you know whom you are serving, you align your QBR to best serve them. UGG figured out that surfers were the whom. Brian's QBR was the delivery of functional footwear. Of all the communities in the world, Brian loved the surfing community. That is who he is. He quickly determined the whom, then spent the necessary time (years, in fact) in improving and improving how he served them. He improved the design. He built and strengthened the relationships with the influencers. He became world famous for his perfect product, in a tiny world. That needs to be your aspiration, too: to become world famous in a select, small world. That small world will then carry you on its shoulders to the bigger world.

THE HOW

So how do you service your *whom*? What do you do that benefits them more than anyone else can benefit them? The core concept is to refine your offering to your best customers until you get something they are ecstatically buying and recommending. And do this the whole time while ensuring you are delivering what is aligned with your QBR.

The QBR is what your company thrives (or dies) by. The how is the way you piece together the QBR, and all of the other elements of your business to deliver what you do, to your clients.

The underwear company Nation Up North (NUN for short) did this. They found a community to serve: chefs. They tested their product, changing the materials and the shape to suit chefs' needs. They discovered the problem that needed fixing more than anything—a little problem called "waiter butt." (I know. It makes the food sound real tasty, right?) Waiters, chefs, and staff sweat a lot. Restaurant kitchens, as a rule, are not air-conditioned well or at all. There is just no effective way to cool a kitchen that is throwing off way more heat than air conditioning could ever handle. So kitchens can be 15 to 20 degrees Fahrenheit hotter than the ambient temperature. The NUN undies, with their design being loose where it needs to be loose and wicking sweat where wicking is critical, resolved "waiter butt."

It took NUN a lot of iterations to get its "waiter butt" undies right. Once it mastered the product, the chef community talked about it. Undies moved off the shelves and onto people's bottoms. NUN was quickly acquired.

Know your QBR first. That is your and your company's heart. Then know the whom. And pair it with the how. You now have your Commitment, and your ability to run a Clockwork business depends on you honoring that commitment.

After I wrote and published my first book, I discovered my authentic *whom*: mom entrepreneurs who were entering or reentering the workforce after their children reached an age that gave them enough freedom to run their own business part-time. Many people suggested my niche was small business owners, but I knew it was all about mom entrepreneurs as I was building my business. Did other people read my book? Absolutely. And I love them for it. (Shout-out to the dudes slogging their way through entrepreneur-land. I see ya, my brothas.) But had I focused on the broader community of small business owners right out of the gate, I wouldn't have been noticed. I lived the lesson Brian Smith taught us: If you want big success, you need to first focus on a small community, and then empower that community to carry you to bigger markets.

Choosing my community affected how I wrote my books, and how I marketed and sold them. When I found where the mom entrepreneurs congregated and showed up—at conferences and retreats hosted by other mom entrepreneurs, like Angela Jia Kim, who were achieving impressive business growth—that community carried me not only to other mom entrepreneurs, but also to other niche groups within the broader community of small business owners. And the best part of all of that strategy was that I grew my audience, and my business, with minimal effort. See how that works?

CLOCKWORK IN ACTION

1. Fill in the *whom* and the *how. Our commitment is to serve [whom] by [how].* Then post this statement on your desk for you to see, and somewhere in your office where everyone can see it.

2. Now that you know how to balance your team, consider who on your team has the right traits or instincts to serve your customer community. Based on this assessment, are they in the right role?

CHAPTER EIGHT

STEP SEVEN: KEEP AN EYE ON YOUR BUSINESS

know an entrepreneur who, once he reached a point where he could stop doing the "grunt work" and focus on managing his staff, said, "Screw doing the work, all I want to do is move the pieces on the chessboard." I didn't like the way he stated that, because it sounded manipulative. He saw people as pawns, and that's total bull. He saw himself as the king and his colleagues as simply part of his fiefdom. Controlling or dictating others does not jibe with me. So don't you dare see your people as pawns on a chessboard. I've got my eye on you.

But what I did like about the chessboard metaphor was the idea of putting the right people in the right roles and guiding them to the right results. A chessboard has different pieces with different capabilities, just as a business has different people and different technologies and different systems, all with different capabilities. A master chess player moves the pieces strategically to achieve the victory. Your job is to put the different pieces in your business in the best places to move your company forward. But a more apt visual is of a dashboard that allows you to keep your thumb on the pulse of your business. A dashboard has simple gauges that show you how you are progressing. Similar to a dashboard in your car— or, if you're feeling fancy, the control panel in an airplane.

In chapter six, you learned how to balance your team so that the right people are doing the right things, in the right portions, right. Your team and their roles, tasks, and 4Ds can be part of your dashboard, for sure. Over the years, I've added metrics to my dashboard and taken others away. Getting your business to run like clockwork is more than just putting people in the right roles; it's about measuring the right aspects of your business so that you'll be able to spot a problem from *outside* the business when something needs tweaking.

If the idea of metrics is getting your undies in a bunch, don't sweat. It is not nearly as daunting as it sounds. You don't need to be a mathematician or engineer. You simply need to pick the critical things you want to measure.

KEEP IT SIMPLE

The simplicity of it all can be shocking. I connected with Kevin Fox, the founder of Viable Vision, a company that specializes in manufacturing efficiency. At the end of the day, every business is a manufacturer, meaning we start with raw goods (or in service-based business, raw ideas) and then assemble those goods to deliver an end product. Manufacturers go through a sequence of steps to make those goods. In short, there is a lot to learn from manufacturers, in particular, manufacturing efficiency. As I spoke with Kevin, he shared powerful stories on how to find the bottlenecks in a business—the points where the business slows down.

Just like a chain, only one link can be the weakest. Once you strengthen that link, another link by default will become the weakest. We need to focus our attention there. But how do you know the weak link is fixed?

"With a metric," explained Kevin. "It doesn't need to be some fancy computer system reporting a flashing number to a flat panel screen in the manager's office. In fact, I recommend simple measurements, things that you can see and evaluate in the moment without the need for calculations or computer algorithms. Something like the blue light measurement."

When Kevin said this, my mind instantly went to the Kmart bluelight specials. Blue lights flashing and people flocking to the racks for the specials being offered. Turns out, I wasn't that far off. Kevin shared a story of a car bumper manufacturer that hired Viable Vision to improve the company's efficiency. Kevin and his team went to the manufacturer to seek out bottlenecks where things were waiting to get done. Sure enough, right in front of the welding station, inventory was piling up, sitting there . . . waiting. Your business's bottlenecks will reveal themselves in the same way. Right before the bottleneck, things will pile up and wait. Time just wastes away.

With the bumpers piling up, Kevin looked at the thing they were waiting for, to be welded. That was the bottleneck. He noticed that the distinct blue light that welding torches put off very rarely fired. Then he simply observed. He noticed that the welders went to the stockpile, carried over the parts, put them in a jig, spot-welded them to hold the parts in position, and then, and only then, fired up the welding torch to weld it all together. Then they cleaned off the parts, moved them to the completed section, and started the process all over again. All in all, the welders were spending about 10 percent of their time actually welding. So the blue lights flickering only happened—you guessed it again—10 percent of the time.

The Primary Job of the welders is to weld. And it was clear, from the lack of blue lights, that their Primary Job was not being prioritized. In fact, they were doing their Primary Job only—you guessed it again—10 percent of the time.

To fix the problem, Kevin simply hired a few teenagers to serve as assemblers. Their job was to move parts and get them ready for the welders. The assemblers would carry the parts to the welder and put them in the jig. The assemblers would then move out any finished parts to the completed section. As the assemblers were doing this, the welder would do the spot welds and then fire up the welding torch and get to work. Blue lights flashing. The assemblers, after moving the completed parts, would walk back to the parts waiting to be welded, where they would assemble the parts in the jig (which had casters on it) and wheel the bumper components to the welder. By this time, the welder had just finished welding the other bumper. The assemblers would put the new jig in position and wheel out the completed bumper. The welder would start welding again, blue lights flashing. A lot.

With this fix, bumpers now started to go through the former bottleneck at lightning speed. The pile of parts was depleted within days, and parts rarely ever piled up again. And the entire business was able to output bumpers faster than ever. The magic wasn't just in the solution, but in the metric. It was really simple— if Kevin saw blue lights flashing constantly, that meant the bottleneck was flowing. But if the lights stopped for any period of time, or flashed much less often, that indicated a problem.

Kevin, and subsequently the owner of the factory, had a ridiculously simple and yet wildly effective metric: Are the blue lights flashing? You should aim to make your metrics as simple as possible, too. You want to measure if business is flowing well. That's it. When it's not, the job of the metric is to simply notify you that there is a problem. And if there is a problem, your job, chess master, is to investigate and fix. Blue lights flashing? All is good. Don't see the blue lights much? That is a signal for you to look for the problem.

Think about your own car's dashboard. As you're driving, you have various gauges you check to make sure everything is A-OK. In one two-second glance, you can tell if you're driving too fast, if your engine is overheating, or if you're running low on gas. These are all simple indicators of a problem, and that action is required.

If you're going too fast, you take your foot off the accelerator. If your engine is overheating, you can pull over and check your coolant levels. (Or if, like me, you are relatively clueless about cars, you pull over and jump out thinking your engine is on fire . . . then get roadside assistance to tell you it was just steam. True story.) If you're running low on gas, you can fill up at the next stop. Without the instruments on your dashboard, you might get pulled over for speeding, watch your engine smoke (for real), or find yourself stranded in the middle of nowhere.

The same is true in business. A dashboard with metrics will show you how critical aspects of your business are doing. Then, if something is out of whack, you can quickly check on the health of your business and make tweaks if necessary. When all of your dashboard metrics are indicating all is well, you can focus on the future of your business and not worry about the day-to-day operation. That's a beautiful thing, because this is when you're making money on autopilot. Yes, that's a real thing. I'm not talking about the "passive income" so many late-night infomercials promise. I'm talking about running the business you love while spending a mere fraction of the time you currently spend doing the work in the business, bringing in more cash than you ever truly thought possible, and loving every minute of it.

ATTRACT, CONVERT, DELIVER, AND COLLECT

Every year, my friends Selena Soo and Chris Winfield (remember him? the former productivity guy?) host eight or nine dinners in New York for a mix of authors, speakers, and experts. Selena and Chris are the ultimate connectors, and their dinner events have quickly become heralded as the who's who of the entrepreneurial educator space. For me, this is the equivalent of the Oscars, just without the requirement of black tie and a lot fewer duck face pictures.

You can't just go to the dinner; you have to be invited. My first invite, two winters back, I threw the "play hard to get" protocol out the window and accepted the invite within milliseconds. Four weeks later, I was making my trek into New York. Dinner kicked off with Selena and Chris showing appreciation for us, their guests. As I took a sip of the incredibly smooth cabernet, I scanned the room of fifteen or so guests. I recognized most of the faces and you would have, too (one of the rules is that the attendee list remains confidential and attendees are revealed only with the hosts' direct permission). "Holy smokes, that's so-and-so from that such-and-such new show," I thought. "Wow, that is the editor of the number one magazine for entrepreneurs." And right across from me was the fabled master of business streamlining . . . Adrienne Dorison.

That night I hung on every word she said about how she made lumberyards more efficient by addressing the countless bottle-necks, such as changing the way trees are loaded in the hauling truck to make them unload faster. How buffer yards helped de-liver a constant feed of lumber and prevented truckers from skip-ping deliveries because of long lines. And how to deal with politics and ego that can slow a lumberyard down to a snail's pace. All these improvements have a small impact. But none of them were necessarily the QBR, by my understanding.

I explained to Adrienne what I had learned about the QBR and gave her my explanation of the impact. She got it and agreed. And as serendipity would have it, she had studied bees for years. Meaning she really understood the importance of the QBR.

"All businesses have bottlenecks, Mike. These are necessary parts of a business that must all be operating with excellence, otherwise the business will suffer. All parts of the business are important to different degrees. In order to deliver its product or service to clients, the essential parts of the business must all work. The most critical of those are the bottlenecks—the areas where production is necessary but slower than what is feeding it. And of all essential parts of the business, the grandfather of them all is the QBR. It is the tide that lifts all boats, so to speak. All the elements of a business can be broken into four quadrants, and the QBR therefore can only exist in one of those four spots: leads or sales or deliverables or cash flow."

"So?" I asked Adrienne. "What is the QBR for lumberyards?"

Adrienne looked at me and stretched her neck to the side as she squinted one eye. You know that look, when someone is surprised you asked the question, since you should know the answer. Then she responded, "You tell me."

I had stumped myself. I paused, thought, and then responded, "Well, it depends, doesn't it?"

"That's right," she said.

I continued. "Of course! The QBR is self-determined. Just like your business, just like my business, just like any business, the industry doesn't determine the QBR. The leader of the business determines what the QBR is. The leader picks what the business will make its stance on. Therefore, the lumberyards you worked with can choose. In fact, they need to choose."

I was on a roll now. "One lumberyard may bank its success on the speed of the operation. They want to make lumber, fast.

And in that case, the QBR is what makes the operation move the fastest. Just like a beehive's QBR is to hatch new bees from eggs. And that is why the Queen Bee is revered, since she makes the eggs."

"Bingo!" said Adrienne. "If the lumberyard declares speed of production as the QBR, they then look on what part of the business operation most influences the speed of production and which people are serving that role. And, so you know, that is what most lumberyards choose as their QBR. Then they usually find that the crane operation is the QBR. If the crane that unloads trucks and puts the wood into the cutting and debarking machines is moving optimally, the business flows, and if not, the business slows."

"Exactly!" I said, excitedly and a little too loudly for the kind of restaurant we were at. "And that means the crane operator is the one serving the QBR. He, just like a doctor, needs to be protected and served."

"You got it, Mike. And don't forget that is just one choice of QBRs. A lumberyard may determine that they will be world famous for their quality of wood. Speed becomes secondary to selection in this case. So the QBR is now identifying the best wood raw materials. The crane operator is still a relevant employee, of course, but they are not serving the QBR. The lumber quality control manager is. They are serving the QBR."

Adrienne was on fire! "But a lumberyard's QBR is not restricted to a deliverable," she continued. "It could also be in the attraction of prospects, or converting them into clients. In fact, one lumber company I worked with put the QBR in the conversion. They built a staff of experts, including engineers, who, during the sales process, guided prospects on making the best value-based decisions and gave this guidance to a degree that far surpassed that of any of their competitors. Cheap wood may save the customer money but fail to serve its intended project and end up having to be replaced with more expensive materials. So while they turned around projects the fastest, and always had the best grade of wood, it was the fact that customers trusted them entirely that contributed to their soaring sales."

Adrienne explained that lumberyards aren't unique, in that every business determines its QBR. And the QBR always sits within one of four quadrants: leads, sales, deliverables, or cash flow. I prefer to think of these aspects of business in terms of things we do, and so I modified them a bit, though the meaning is the same: Attract, Convert, Deliver, Collect (ACDC). (Recall that I first mentioned ACDC in chapter five.)

Adrienne and I talked the night away and I learned that every business has these four quadrants, and whenever a business is experiencing inefficiencies, it is going to be that the QBR is not being properly protected or served, or there is a bottleneck in the ACDC.

Adrienne's insight blew my mind. Let me break down what I learned for you:

1. **Attract.** Every business needs to attract prospects, or leads, which are inquiries into your product or service. Leads feed your sales. No leads and your sales will dry up, because you have no one to sell to.
2. **Convert.** The responsibility of sales is to *convert* a lead into a paying customer. You may have all the leads in the world, but if you can't convert them into sales, your business is going under.
3. **Deliverables.** Deliverables are the processes and services necessary to properly deliver on what you sold the customer. If you don't deliver on what the customer buys, they will seek a way out . . . sometimes canceling their

order, sometimes seeking a refund, possibly spreading the word about how you stink. Can't deliver? You can't stay in business.

4. **Collect.** If the customer doesn't deliver on their promise to pay you, you are in trouble. If you don't collect the money for the work you do or can't keep the money (because the customer takes it back or you blow it), you are out of business.

THE ACDC MODEL

These are the core four functions of every business. You must do them all well. And as we get on to playing the famous game all good business leaders play, "bottleneck whack-a-mole," you will constantly evaluate and fix all the things big and small within these four areas, just like Adrienne did for the lumberyard. Almost all businesses follow the ACDC predictable path of sustainability, in the same sequence. First, you must generate interest in your offering (Attract leads). Then, for the people interested, you must convince them to buy from you (Convert leads to sales). Once they are a customer, you must Deliver on your promise. At some point during the process, you must take money from them for the work you do (Collect).

However, there are a few unique cases. For example, some businesses do work "on spec," in which the deliverable is completed before the prospect becomes a customer. In this case, the flow would be ADCC.

Collecting cash can be seen a little bit as a wild card. You, for example, may collect it before you even start the work (the deliverable). But even if you have collected the money before you did the work, it is not really yours until after you deliver on your promise to your client. If you don't, the customer may request their money back. You know, by suing you. This is why I put the categories in this sequence and why you need at least one metric for each category. This is how you can see the flow of clients through your business.

Let me show you my own dashboard for Profit First Professionals.

1. **ATTRACT.** Your metric for attracting leads may be how many people have completed a specific action. For an online training program, it could be how many people are giving their email address to you in exchange for your free giveaway. For a B2B (business to business), it could be how many people ask for a proposal. For Profit First Professionals (PFP), it's how many people have filled out our initial application form on our website. If we get three people a day completing that form, that translates to a little more than one thousand applications a year (three leads a day times 365 days). When they fill it out and submit it, we acknowledge it as a lead. When fewer people are filling out a form, that triggers a question. The metric doesn't say that our form isn't working, but that could be the issue. It tells us that we have *some* kind of issue, because fewer people are filling out the form. This triggers us to investigate and resolve the problem. Just as when your check engine light comes on, you know that you need to get a diagnostic. It could be noth-

ing big (a loose wire) or it could be big (a busted transmission). When we see our metric fall short of our expectation of three per day, our question is, "Why aren't more people filling out our form?" The answer could be because our website is down, or because people are calling us instead, or we have an issue with the QBR (the messenger of Profit First) and nothing is trickling out on the other side, which means we need to find and fix a bottleneck.

2. **CONVERT.** Our metric for converting leads into sales is the number of people who join us as new members within three months of originating as a lead. It's a simple percentage: We want a 33 percent conversion rate, which will bring in approximately 360 new members a year. That being said, not all prospects are made the same (you know what I am talking about). Some leads are ideal, some are total tire kickers, others are too early in their business to be a fit, and so on. Some qualitative discussions that come up during our quarterly meetings are how to message better, how to bring in better qualified leads, and how to sell better so we can more quickly separate out the ideal fits from the misfits. The metrics are simply dashboard indicators of performance, but we (and you should) dig in deeper to make even more impactful decisions. The way this metric works, we know that if we talk to one hundred people during a month, and only ten become members (10 percent instead of 33 percent), something may be askew. Likewise, if eighty become members (as glorious as that sounds), something else may be askew. The metric simply tells you whether something is different than expected. When

that happens, you need to investigate.* Well outside our 33 percent conversion? We ask ourselves, "What's going on with sales?" Did we introduce a new pricing structure that didn't work? Did we hire a new sales team member? Is the quality of leads changing? We also look back up the chain. Before conversions is leads, so if we have a red flag with conversions, we ask, "Do we have a slowdown in the leads metric, too?" If so, the problem is likely leads and we investigate there first.

3. **DELIVER.** Do you deliver on what the customer expects (or better)? For some businesses, the best indicator of nailing the deliverables is that customers come back again and again (retention). Another is when customers rave about the experience, therefore enabling marketing by word of mouth. Maybe, if you have lower standards, it is the lack of complaints. For example, think of a rest stop on a highway. Surely it has happened, but I think that people rarely post "I just took the most glorious whiz at the most remarkable rest stop ever" or "You have just got to see these urinal cakes. Out. Of. This. World!" If people have anything to say about a rest stop, it's usually a complaint. So the fewer complaints, the better.

   At PFP, our deliverables are measured by completed milestones. One of those milestones is certification. This

---

* Sometimes the gauge in any of these metrics will stay the same, yet there still is a problem. Your sales conversion stays at 33 percent, but you are only making one sale a month. That means the problem is likely leads, where, sure enough, there are only three leads that month. But it can be worse. You might have all the leads you expect, and all the conversions, but the new clients are impossible to retain. A problem like this might reveal itself with a retention metric (showing turnover), but the problem may be the lead quality. Meaning, sometimes the problem reveals itself elsewhere (retention), but the cause is not there (in this case, leads). Take a lesson from roof repairs. Just because the water leak is coming into your home at the wall, the hole in the roof can be somewhere totally different. Occasionally, problems travel around before they reveal themselves.

is because I know that once a person gets certified in Profit First, they have completed a sequence of training through PFP and have been adequately trained to pass that test. I know that if people get the certificate, they have mastered the process in their business and are ready to serve clients. Our metric is how many people have completed their certification within six months of signing up. We want that metric to be 97 percent. While we would love to have 100 percent as our metric, that is not realistic (unforeseen circumstances do happen, such as life events). And aiming for 100 percent means that we would be in a constant red flag situation. Oh, no, we are not at 100 percent again, what happened? Since it is unachievable, we will never get there, which means we will begin to ignore it.

The lesson here is, don't make your metrics "dream numbers"; make them realistic indicators. As I write this, that metric for our member certification is at about 90 percent. That's lower than expected, and I know that means that members are possibly not engaged in some way. Are we falling short on our support to them, or have they lost interest? I need to figure it out, since I am sure that at least that missing 7 percent will be less engaged, or less prepared, or need extra attention to catch up.

4. **COLLECT.** Repeat after me: Cash is the lifeblood of my business. Again. Cash is the lifeblood of my business. Cash is the most important yet most overlooked part of every business. You could not have a single good client, your services could be horrible, and you could be clueless about how to generate leads, but if you have wads of cash, your business will survive. In our organization, we look for the percentage of members who miss a payment

during any given month. If that is over 5 percent, we have an issue. Any time we can make it lower (and we found that offering an annual payment program did) we are feeding our business the lifeblood of cash it needs to sustain. How is cash flowing (or not flowing) through your business? Determine the metric that you can use to measure its health. Your business life depends on it.

5. **Queen Bee Role.** Our QBR is getting the word out about Profit First, and I am the primary (but not exclusive) messenger. The metric for our QBR is how many presentations are happening—speeches, keynotes, webinars, podcasts (our own, or someone else's)—or interviews. And our QBR is strengthening. As I write this (on a plane, per usual) four Profit First speeches are happening without me. We are measuring the number of "messaging moments" each day. It would be nice to know the audience size, of course. A live event is much more measurable than a podcast. And a podcast is more measurable than a radio interview. So we just measure the number of messaging moments. We have our metric set at two messaging moments per day (fourteen a week), which if I have to do solo, is doable, but barely. And if I get sick, we are in trouble.

As more people are serving the QBR, that number has become more consistent and I am working less (you know, money on automatic). My personal service of the QBR (I track my work, too) of late is down because I've been busy with other projects (hello, writing a book is time consuming!), which detract from the QBR. But as I free the queen (me), other people are carrying the QBR forward. Although writing a book does serve the QBR in the long term, since it's technically me getting the word out, publishing is a long process, so writing—and rewriting, and editing, and editing some more, and then throwing everything out and starting again (seriously)—is not reflected in this metric. The other folks who are serving the QBR are working well, so now my priority is to build a system to make it as easy as possible for them and for others who also want to speak, while ensuring consistency. And I am doing it by, you guessed it, capturing the existing system: recording my presentations and giving them to folks to present.

The core four areas—Attract, Convert, Deliver, and Collect (ACDC)—become the gauges on your dashboard—plus the QBR. What you need to do is first identify *how* you measure progress (or lack thereof) in each of these five spots, and what is your goal for each. The goal of metrics is to measure the effectiveness of your company, and likely areas to find bottlenecks. The metrics act as a simple initial indicator that something is askew and needs your attention.

A metric is usually a number. It can also be a binary (yes/no or on/off), or it can be something else. But a metric is always measurable and comparable. A metric sets the expectations, and when the actual events that the metric is measuring are higher or lower than expected, it indicates that an investigation of the situation is appropriate, and a resolution may be required.

Going back to our car example, the car's speed could be the metric we measure. The speed limit sign could be the "normal" number we want, and the speedometer indicates the actual number. When we go too fast or too slow, there is an inconsistency with the metric and an adjustment needs to be considered. (But trust me, no one drives too slow in New Jersey.)

In any category, you can have the opportunity for multiple

metrics. For example, we also have a convocation metric in deliverables. Convocation is how many members join us for an in-person live training at our headquarters after they join our organization. It is not just critical training; it is critical interaction. New members meet one another and the team at home base (that is what we call the main offices). If members aren't showing up for convocation, that may set the stage for problems with long-term engagement. The metric is a simple ratio: how many members qualify to be at convocation (which is any new member) versus how many actually show.

The Profit First method works in part because it has built-in metrics—it is its own dashboard for managing cash and ensuring your business is profitable. The goal is to have a business that both generates and sustains cash and profit. In *Profit First,* I explain that you need five foundational bank accounts: INCOME, PROFIT, OWNER'S COMPENSATION, TAX, and OPERATING EXPENSES. Then you start allocating funds based on preestablished percentages (which serve as metrics, too) for each of the five accounts. Money comes in and is distributed according to those percentages. If your business can't allocate money to the percentages set, those percentages serve as a metric, an indicator that something out of the range of expectation is happening, and you need to find out why the business can't do the allocations, and fix it. Do you have too much cost? Cash flow problem? Not enough margin? The fluctuation in numbers from what is expected indicates you either have a problem (you fell short) or things are going better than you expected (you landed high). In either scenario, you always want to ask why. And seek to fix the bad things and replicate the good things. Metrics are your new best friend; they candidly tell you the truth about any issues or opportunities you have and point you in the direction of a solution—quickly.

The notion of money on automatic doesn't mean money falls into your lap without any effort. It's not a broken ATM that somehow got jammed and perpetually spits money out at you. Instead, money on automatic is establishing a system where you sit back in the control room and watch the flow. Just like any machine, system, or process, it will break at times or need adjustments. Your job is to watch for the anomalies and then seek to resolve them. The key is to have as simple a control room as possible, yet have it monitor the critical elements in your business. Could you have a metric for everything? Sure. But that would be overwhelming. Could you have just one metric? Sure. But it may be too vague to indicate problems and opportunities.

For example, with Profit First, you set an expected income metric on a biweekly (or weekly) basis. Even a seasonal business can do this, too. Then you compare where you are on that income versus where you expected to be. Something is off? You investigate. You don't have to read cash flow statements or other reports to see if your business is in need of cash or profit is down.

Craig Merrills and I met at a conference where I was presenting. We quickly became friends. He and his wife were so incredibly generous to share their vacation house on Smith Mountain Lake, Virginia, with my wife, Krista, and me. We spent a few days together playing cornhole (the ultimate outdoor game that you can play without putting your beer down), firing up the BBQ, and chatting up a storm about all things business.

Craig runs a Wow 1 Day Painting franchise. He had an uncanny ability to borrow money and justified it because he needed equipment. The result was $109,000 of debt. That's when Craig put in a few simple metrics to turn things around. He simply set his income target and the percentage of operating expenses (including the purchase of equipment) that he could spend. With a constant percentage of operating expenses, if income slipped, the operating expense automatically received a smaller portion. He only spent money that was pre-allocated to expenses.

Craig started this process only a year and one month prior to our meetup at his lake house. He threw in yet another three-pointer on cornhole, took a swig of his beer, looked at me, and said, "Now, I am totally debt free."

He eradicated his debt because he measured it. He doesn't read accounting statements; he uses the key metrics on his dashboard to measure cash flow and free up funds to pay down his debt. You may have heard this before, but either way, I hope it lands with you: What gets measured gets done. So, if it matters, measure it.

You don't necessarily have to follow my categories or metrics for your dashboard, but I do suggest you have metrics that show indicators throughout your business. Also, try to key your dashboard to somewhere between five and eight metrics. Fewer than that, and you don't get a full enough picture of what's going on. But more than that can be overwhelming. Too many dials and too many "instruments" make it difficult for you to notice when something isn't working, which defeats the purpose of having a dashboard.

Imagine a security guard on the night shift. The guard can stare at six different screens and easily spot the slightest movement. But give that guard *six hundred* screens and you can be sure that he will miss something. Every movie where that bad guy gets past the security guard watching the monitors is because the guard has too many freaking monitors . . . or got distracted by the "suspicious noise" of that metal object the bad guy just threw down the hallway. (It always works like a charm.) A dashboard allows you to be the security guard for your business, so the fewer metrics to monitor, the better. And, for God's sake, don't fall for the "noise down the hallway" trick—it's always a trap.

ONE DIAL AT A TIME

My lawnmower stopped mowing the summer I started writing this book. It began sputtering randomly, and instead of cutting the grass, it was lightly fanning it—moving the grass from one side to the other. Off to the garage I went to repair this beast once and for all, and I immediately committed the cardinal sin. I tried to fix all the possible causes at once. I cleaned the carburetor, replaced the air filter, changed the oil, and refueled it, all at one time. Then I tried to start the engine. This time, it ran worse.

Since none of my efforts fixed the problem, I readied myself for extreme engine repair. I gave it new belts, new spark plugs, and flushed the engine with a cleaner. Sure enough, it didn't work. Finally, after two days of working on the mower, I brought it into a shop. Thirty minutes later it was fixed. The problem? The carburetor was damaged, presumably by me. (I won't confirm or deny jamming the cover back into place when it wouldn't close properly.) The original problem was likely a clogged air filter. But even though I fixed that, I "fixed" other things at the same time, which actually caused a new problem, which I mistakenly concluded was the same as the original problem.

The point is, when you work on multiple things at once to fix one problem, you may actually fix and unfix the solution all in one shot, not realizing that you actually had fixed it and what the cause was. The solution is to work on one piece at a time, and see if that fixes the problem. Start with the most likely issue, test it, and then move to the next likely issue.

The dashboard of our business is our process. At times things will fail, and when that happens we need to turn (fix) one dial at a time. Take sales for example. Let's say you notice that you have a big sales drop-off. You notice that lead flow has not changed much at all, and, if anything, has increased, but the sales team is selling way less. You hired a new salesperson who is coming up to speed, and you see that their sales are far lower than you expect. So you set out to fix it. You turn the next "dial" on your dashboard: you give them a new sales script to follow. You give them more leads than the rest of the team, so they can cut their teeth faster. Instead of one of your experienced people giving sales training, you now have two working with the new guy, in the hopes they will gain even more knowledge. With all the fixes in place, sales are sure to increase. But they drop further. Why? Is it the script? Is this person handling too many leads at once? Or maybe the salesperson is too intimidated when two people are watching over their shoulder.

Rewind and start again. Sales are slower since the new guy started. You conclude that the two things are probably related. You go to the obvious thing, the script, and just turn that dial. You change the script to an easier version. Then you observe. Sales don't move up or down. Now you go back to the prior sales script, setting the dial back to its original setting, and then move the next dial. Thinking it has something to do with the training, you try two salespeople working with the new guy. As before, sales don't increase, but in fact drop sharp and fast. Interesting. You found a dial that is negatively affecting sales. Now you investigate this oddity.

When you go back to just one salesperson mentoring the new guy, sales go up but stay lower than your historical average. Then you try the crazy idea of eliminating the role of sales mentor, and sales go back to normal. Weird. Now you know exactly what is causing your problem, and you do a deep investigation. You discover that your sales mentors, when working with the new salesperson, were putting off their own sales calls. Prospects were calling the mentors and waiting and waiting for a response. So you change the mentoring work to happen after hours and improve it with the use of some technology—recording calls. Now your best salespeople are closing deals, and then going over the recordings of those calls with the new salesperson after hours. And guess what? Sales skyrocket.

Sometimes, when you spot a problem on your dashboard in one category, the problem can be emanating from another. For example, the challenge with collections is that some people get paid before they actually do the work. That's great, but if your business has a cash flow issue, is it really a collections issue? When you look at your dashboard, you might see that your sales are down and your leads metrics are right on point. What could that mean? Perhaps because wannabe customers are required to pay up front, no one is buying. The fix? Testing one dial at a time. Try removing the upfront payment requirement and see what happens. If things go back to your expectations, you found the cause. But if it doesn't fix it, then—and this is the key—put the upfront payment requirement back and then go for the next fix. You have to test each dial independently to find the cause.

When you turn multiple dials that affect a common outcome at the same time, you cloud the solution. First one change could fix it and another could counteract it, so even though you had fixed it you undid the fix and don't even know. Other times you change multiple dials and it does fix the problem, but you don't know which one was the fix. Other times you turn multiple dials and nothing fixes it, but now you are unsure if something did fix it and you also undid the fix with another dial . . . or if none of it fixed anything. Turn one dial at a time—the most likely candidate first—and then measure the result. Reset that dial and try another and measure that. Turn the dials in sequence until you find the cause, and only after you do the single dial turns, consider multiple dial turns where a contingency may be in place requiring multiple dials to be turned to fix it.

The key is to move linearly through this process, turning only one dial at a time, from the most likely suspect to the least, until you find the permanent resolution. If you try to turn multiple dials at once, regardless of the outcome, you won't know which dial influenced it. Based on the results, decide which dial to turn next, which in some cases may be a further crank of the dial you just turned.

Moving one dial at a time seems very time consuming. So the question that begs to be asked is, "Can you ever turn more than one dial at a time?" When analyzing a specific outcome where the dials potentially influence a common outcome, most often the answer is no. You must move one dial at a time. But when your company is working on different outcomes, and the dials are disparate from one another (meaning they address different outcomes), you can turn multiple dials at the same time. For example, I may identify that I have a Convert bottleneck that needs to be addressed and want to try turning the dial of revisiting past prospects that didn't convert. And I may also have a Deliver bottleneck that has customers waiting to talk with an implementation specialist, and I want to try turning the dial of doing group sessions for implementation instead of one on one. Those are distinct dials that affect distinct outcomes, so I can try both simultaneously. That's a specific opportunity we had in my business, and we turned both of those dials at the same time. And each one improved its specific outcome.

I know this may seem like a lot of dial turnin', and you may question your ability to recognize when some aspects of your business need to be tweaked, but you've got this. You *do*.

FIXING THE GOOD PROBLEMS

I don't typically do business calls at one in the morning, but some business crises require immediate attention. I had just arrived on a late-night flight to Berlin, Germany, to deliver a keynote on Profit First and was skimming email half-asleep when I noticed one from Cyndi Thomason with a subject line that read "Gasping for Air!," which got my attention. The opening line of her email woke me right up: "I'm numb; truth is I'm overwhelmed with opportunity." I emailed her back to schedule an emergency call. The seven-hour time difference was in Cyndi's favor, so one a.m. was go time.

The QBR is a powerful force. Like the force Luke Skywalker used to lift his X-wing fighter out of the swamp. Once you realize that you can move mountains without doing the work, it can cause you to get a little, or a lot, overwhelmed. Cyndi experienced this firsthand, as the closing paragraph of her email revealed:

"Mike, this niche stuff works, and the QBR works, my worker bees are serving clients like crazy and I'm doing my QBR marketing role. The problem is I don't have enough worker bees, so does the Queen Bee take a vacation? I'm not sure whether to put the brakes on marketing and I've had two other vendors in the space reach out and want me to contribute content.

"These are wonderful problems, but I'm not equipped to solve them. Can you guys help point me in the right direction?"

I've shared Cyndi's journey throughout this book, and you might remember that she had always seemed unflappable. On this call, though, Cyndi's voice was noticeably strained. "I can't keep up with the demand. I can't provide the level of service I'm known for, for all of those leads."

Nailing the QBR is the tide that rises all boats. The QBR is the foundation of your business on which everything else stands.

Cape Cod Hospital's QBR is doctors doing examinations. It is the priority and it is protected. So what happens? The hospital builds a reputation for being the one emergency room you go to and get seen instantly. And that, in turn, opens the floodgates. Patients, just like my sister's husband, drive past other hospitals to make the long trip to go to Cape Cod Hospital.

Cyndi serves e-commerce sellers. Their cash flow is extremely complex. Money flies all over the place, and Cyndi's QBR is taking all the craziness that is going on and communicating it to them in a way that is simple, understandable, and calming. Her customers fell in love with Cyndi's company because they finally found someone who could communicate with them and solve their unique problems. Someone who understands them inside and out (the power of a niche) and delivers exactly what they need (the power of the QBR).

Once they found Cyndi, many of her clients started spreading the word about her company. This is what happens when you serve the QBR. The result of that bragging? For the years that Cyndi was a generalist bookkeeper, she got about one lead a month. When she committed to a niche and targeted her marketing to that niche, over time she ramped to generating one lead a day. That alone is remarkable. Then, when she committed to the QBR and all the things that go with it, she turned up the heat to generate one lead every hour. That level of amplification will make even the most unflappable person gasp for air.

On the call, Cyndi explained what had happened. Because of her reputation, the host of a popular webinar series for Amazon sellers asked her to come on the show and share strategies for managing cash.

"Within an hour of the listing that I was *going* to be on the show, my lead flow jumped," Cyndi told me. Some Amazon sellers had already heard about Cyndi from other e-commerce sellers.

When they saw her name listed on the web series' site, they reached out to ask her about her services. This lead flow, plus the lead generation of the quickly ramping word of mouth, brought her more than twenty-five leads each day.

By 1:15 a.m., I understood the details behind the problem. With the QBR nailed, the flow of leads was cranking. The Attract in ACDC was flowing fast. But that river of prospects was now hitting a bottleneck at the Convert stage. Cyndi couldn't convert all the leads into clients fast enough. People were inquiring about bookkeeping, and then were kept waiting. She could manage it with a little bit of dancing around when the lead flow was one per day. But now at one lead every hour, forget it. Disaster pending. Possible reputation damage.

So for the next forty-five minutes, we worked on fixing the bottleneck. There are a few things you can do in a case like this. For example, find a way to get more prospects through faster. You could hire salespeople, or automate the conversion process with a video sales pitch. For Cyndi's business, we chose neither. We talked about her vision for the company, and then reverse engineered back to the bottleneck.

Cyndi told me about the clients she wanted to serve and the revenue and profit target she intended. We took her revenue/profit target long term, and asked, "What needs to happen this year to make it a reality?" That gave us the twelve-month revenue/profit target.

Then I asked, "How many clients do you want to work with to make it happen?" Cyndi determined one hundred clients was the right size—big enough so that no one client would represent more than 5 percent of total revenue, but small enough that Cyndi would know each and every customer, and, if she desired, could communicate with them all.

Every customer needed to yield $8,000 a year, this year, to

achieve the outcome Cyndi intended. In other words, when she converted a lead to a customer, if that new customer only generated, say, $3,000 of revenue that year, she would not be able to achieve the outcome she wanted. Maybe the customer is winning, because they are working with the world's best e-commerce bookkeeper, after all, but Cyndi wouldn't be able to reach her goals.

Knowing that Cyndi's conversion threshold was $8,000 a year, we communicated that immediately through an email response. Starting at two that morning, one hour after I first read Cyndi's SOS email, when people applied as a lead, leads no longer received the automated email response that read: "Thank you for your interest, we will schedule a call." Now, all leads received this response:

Hi [Contact First Name],

Thank you very much for your interest in bookskeep and for sharing information about your business and your needs.

Our company is a small organization. Our president, Cyndi, and her husband (and business partner), Dave, oversee every one of our accounts. To sustain the highest level of service that our clients expect (and we demand from ourselves), it is necessary that we limit the number of clients we serve. The typical client of ours invests approximately $8,000 a year in our services. I respectfully wanted to share this with you so you can determine if this investment (noting that once we evaluate your needs, the actual pricing might be higher or lower) meets your expectations.

If the anticipated investment is within your expectations, please advise me so that we can schedule a call. I would love to set up a time for us to visit about how bookskeep might be of service to you. Please use the meeting scheduler link below to set up a meeting at a convenient time for you:

[Schedule a Meeting with Bree]

If you are seeking a lower-cost option, may I suggest you consider our monthly webinar series, where we offer profit advising and in-house bookkeeping education. If you are interested in this lower-cost option, please let me know and I can tell you more.

Thank you again for reaching out to bookskeep and always take your profit first!

Bree

(Notice who that automated email comes from? Bree! Remember her? Cyndi moved her into the right role, and doing the sales call is part of it.)

Bottleneck solved. Within a day, the flow of leads stayed the same, but the customers self-vetted, and Cyndi's team only spent time with the properly suited leads. Business flowed stronger and healthier than ever.

Cyndi already knows where the next bottleneck is starting to appear. It is Delivery. Bigger and better customers keep flowing in, and they all want and deserve the highest quality service. So Cyndi is busily designing processes to ensure better and better delivery of service—one dial at a time.

WHEN YOUR QUEEN BEE ROLE IS CLEAR, METRICS WILL SET YOU FREE

Remember Lisé Kuecker's story? She opened Anytime Fitness franchises when her husband was deployed. Lisé started her first business in the second grade. She made coloring sheets for her classmates and sold them for one dollar a book. Being an entrepreneur comes naturally to Lisé, and yet, when she first started out in the fitness industry, she had an all too familiar story. She had contracted with a Fortune 100 company to develop its Pilates and yoga programs, and despite long hours and successful outcomes, she rarely took home a paycheck. Then Lisé decided to take a leap of faith and buy three territories from a young fitness franchise, Anytime Fitness. This time, she didn't plan to work eighty hours a week. Nope. Once she had each location up and running, she planned to work as little as possible.

Lisé opened the first location with her six-month-old son trailing behind her in his walker. Then she opened two more. Then two more. As "crazy" as it sounds, she is a master of applying Parkinson's Law, which we discussed in chapter one. She took on more and more business while her husband was deployed. And without the time to work, she had to make the business work for her. You know, just like clockwork.

As you may recall, all of her locations were in different states than the one she was living in at the time, and even with that challenge (*cough*, opportunity, *cough*), Lisé made it work. She had a meticulous strategy that covered every aspect of running her business, and a system of tracking progress—which I will explain in just a sec.

Within a few years, Lisé's five locations generated multiple seven figures in annual revenue—and she ran all of the locations from her home, working no more than five hours per week. Yes, I am still amazed by that number! I might say it again. Maybe even right now. Lisé would typically spend about a month in a location getting it ready, but once it was up and running, she only spent *five hours a week* running *all five locations*. She and her husband sold their gyms, and now Lisé helps entrepreneurs grow their own businesses using the methods she developed and refined while running her franchises.

To say I was psyched to talk to Lisé would be an understatement. When we spoke on the phone, she immediately shared how she set up her own dashboard so that she could run her business "on automatic." Lisé used . . . wait for it . . . wait for it . . . two dashboards. The first was a weekly spreadsheet that pulled data inputted by every single employee who had a sales role, in all five locations. Whether it was the general manager of a facility, a personal training manager, or a trainer who managed their own sales, they all inputted data every week that funneled into the same report.

The weekly spreadsheet included several key metrics related to gym memberships: new sales, renewals, cancellations, and any type of freezes put into place for members. The snapshot also tracked daily activity, such as how many appointments were made, how many phone calls were received, how many walk-ins came in. Finally, it tracked each location's sales closing percentage.

"It was a powerful spreadsheet," Lisé told me. "But it only took five minutes to go over it, since it had master metrics (seven metrics, to be exact) that gave the pulse. Then I could dig deep on any indicator of a problem. Additionally, my district manager would look at the weekly metrics and then, in our Monday morning meeting, she would report on what she saw in those weekly numbers." So Lisé wasn't looking at her dashboard all week long; her district manager was tracking it. Lisé only looked at the summary weekly dashboard for a few minutes each week. From that information, she could tell if she needed to make an improvement somewhere.

"My Monday meeting was with six core team members—I still do that today as a consultant for the businesses we sold. I would listen to their view of what was happening, and then provide them with guidance and encouragement. Depending on the time of year, I might do a second meeting, but never for more than half an hour. It's a simple numbers review. The numbers don't lie," Lisé explained. "During the meeting, the district manager will explain the circumstances behind the numbers. She might say, 'I know that number is down, but Brittany's husband was just deployed, so that's what's going on right now.'"

Lisé could then tell if a number was falling off due to a temporary situation, such as an employee dealing with the stress of her husband's deployment, or if the metrics represented a bigger problem that needed to be addressed.

"At the end of the month, I got a mass metric sheet. Beyond my dashboard that had the key indicators, each month I would dig deep into all the numbers," Lisé explained. "It was a very simple spreadsheet. One line was our projected goals for the entire year. The next line was last year's numbers for the same goals. And the next line was how we were doing in terms of meeting those goals right now. We could tell where we came from, where we thought we were going, where we expected to go next month, and how we were really doing at that time.

"I could look at last year's attrition numbers for July, for example, and then compare them to July this year and determine what we need to tweak to get that metric closer to where we wanted it to be," Lisé continued. "When you are making goals and projections for your business, many of the shifts are circumstantial—especially as your team grows. You may lose an employee, or something may drop off. The numbers can shift rapidly, and this dashboard allowed me to see the whole picture."

Remember, Lisé was only at the actual gym location in the beginning, but it was during those formative weeks that she would make sure that everyone knew the QBR and how to deliver it. "I had a big vision for what I wanted the gyms to look like, and I understood that I had to inspire that vision in my team," Lisé said. She also made sure she communicated the gym's QBR to existing members, and to people in the community. And, no surprise, she hired based on the QBR. A gym manager who can run a tight ship, but is a jerk, is not helpful. A gym manager who will do whatever they can to deliver extraordinary customer service, but struggles at times with keeping things running smoothly, is okay. The QBR always comes first.

Would Lisé have been able to run her businesses—from another state—working only five hours a week (after the initial location setup) if she wasn't clear about her QBR? If she hadn't trained her staff to deliver on that QBR? And if her customers didn't feel as if they could rely on that QBR? And if she didn't have a strong dashboard to keep her apprised throughout? No way. Further, it was Lisé's passion for changing the obesity rate that kept her motivated, and the success stories she received from members kept her fulfilled, despite her distance from the locations.

Recently, my father had a health scare that scared the living bejeezus out of our family. As he was rushed to the hospital, he was immediately put on certain machines to measure critical vital signs. His pulse, blood pressure, and temperature were monitored. While none of those were his immediate problem, they are critical to life and therefore were monitored. His "bottleneck" was diagnosed by its symptoms: extreme weakness, dehydration, hallucinations. The belief was that it could be a stroke or a urinary tract infection (which manifests in the elderly with symptoms like those he was experiencing). The test showed a urinary tract infection, and he was put on antibiotics. Metrics were put in place, and his health recovered slowly but surely. And the metrics showed that his health improved as the urinary tract infection went away. Two weeks later we all celebrated my pop's ninetieth birthday, with the big guy blowing out the candles with one sturdy exhale. If the metric measurements were not in place, I can only imagine the horrible consequences.

With a clearly defined QBR and a team focused on ensuring that the QBR is delivered consistently, without fail, you too can monitor the health of your business using a dashboard made up of simple metrics. You must have numbers that tell you the normal expectations for the four core parts of your business: Attracting (leads), Converting (sales), Delivering (your promise), and Collecting (their promise). The numbers don't lie. But they don't tell you the whole story, either. They simply flag an opportunity to fix or amplify something. With the metric flag raised, take action and investigate. You can finally fully step away from your business and manage by the numbers. And you can still experience joy and fulfillment as you grow your business. Even if you only work a few hours a week.

 ## CLOCKWORK IN ACTION

Take twenty minutes right now and determine the core metrics you want to use to create your own dashboard. Remember to keep it simple; it's too hard to track too many things. Set your smartphone alarm or timer for twenty minutes, and just get started with identifying those core metrics—those few things that best pinpoint the health of your business.

The ideal metrics to create always include a way to measure QBR performance, as well as the bottleneck(s) you have identified with the ACDC. What are the key things you think you can do to increase the flow through your ACDC? Classify those metrics and measure the progress over time. Where do you think your business is at the most risk when there is a problem in the ACDC? What dimensions of the business are you trying to improve? Determine metrics to help you monitor those things.

Still struggling, or want to bring in an expert to help you fully design a business that runs itself, one that *runs like clockwork?* I am happy to report that my meetup with Adrienne Dorison flourished into a business partnership. Together, we formed Run Like Clockwork, a comprehensive framework designed to assist you and your team in streamlining any and every part of your business. If you want to learn how we can help you, go to RunLikeClockwork.com.

CHAPTER NINE

PUSHBACK
(AND WHAT TO DO ABOUT IT)

My most recent speaking tour in Australia was an unexpected equivalent of taking a four-week vacation. I was working on this book at the time and I was in the midst of testing the Clockwork process on my own business. I think this is what makes my work somewhat atypical compared to that of some other authors and consultants. When I research a concept, I first test it on my business, often for years, before I start to write about it. And then, during the writing process, I continue to test the system on other businesses and test tweaks on mine. It is a very iterative process.

After enjoying the smorgasbord breakfast, including world-class pastries, at the iconic, albeit old-fashioned, Miss Maud Hotel in Perth, I sipped on coffee and opened my laptop, right there at the table. I thought of a final tweak to the system after having a conversation with Australian entrepreneur Leticia Mooney earlier in the week. Once I had made that one last improvement, I was done with the core of the book and had nothing left to do. I considered a second round at the smorgasbord, but that would only result in extra tires around the waistline. Twiddling my thumbs, I wondered what I could do. I checked email. Nothing. Refreshed. Still nothing. If you've ever experienced the stress of an overflowing inbox, it doesn't come anywhere near the terror I felt at looking at an empty one. In that moment, I had a realization: I thought I had finally moved past the biggest barrier to ensuring my businesses ran on its own—my ego. But, alas, I had not.

In Perth, I was literally on the other side of the world—almost directly opposite on the globe from my home in New Jersey. The time difference between the two places is twelve hours, so my day was their night and vice versa. This meant my team slept while I worked the day away in Australia. And when they were awake and cranking it in Jersey, I was asleep and dreaming of shrimp on the barbie. With the extreme time difference, if my team needed anything, they couldn't immediately get ahold of me, nor could I get ahold of them.

After a couple of days of this, I began to feel as though the world didn't need me. It was the ultimate disconnect. The difference between freedom and not being needed was stark. Really, it was a bucket of cold water to the face. I always wanted to be free of my business, but no one calling me, not even to ask for my credit card to pay for the office pizza party. Well, jeez, that was tough to accept. My team wasn't just running the business; they were running it without me. I had spent years designing a company that could run on its own, and now I had *proof* that I'd pulled it off. The realization that I was not needed? That just tore into my soul.

Alone again at my table, the downward spiral of thoughts kicked in. I was alone in Australia, locked in solitary confinement by a wall of Danishes and apple turnovers, and no one at my office even cared. I mean, not a soul needed me. Cue: Panic! Would they even notice if I went on a walkabout in the outback and never came back?

So what did I do? The only thing a human being faced with their own dispensability would do: I reinserted myself into the business. I started sending emails with questions and requests. I made busywork for myself and others. I started throwing wrenches into the well-oiled machine I created. As soon as my team in Jersey woke up, they saw dozens of emails from me, all of which made my team slow down, start stumbling on tasks, and seeking my input on how to proceed. It instantly made my schedule in Australia that much more demanding. Brilliant, right? If you think even for a second my decision was smart, just picture me. There I am, sitting with a smorgasbord of food around me, surrounded by Australian grandmas (who apparently like to frequent Miss Maud), barking out commands in voicemails to my team, and as a result, hampering my own company.

Let's be clear on this: I've never claimed to be the smartest tool in the shed. A tool, maybe. Okay, I was definitely a tool. This was not about my brains, this was about my ego. This was about human nature. You may have experienced a similar need to remain relevant in your own business, or in other aspects of your life. Maybe when you sent your kids off to college. I know my wife and I felt that. All of a sudden, a house of commotion became an empty warehouse of "now what?" First, you get the amazing "this is the first day of my life" feeling of relief when they walk out the door. Then, when dinnertime rolls around, and there's no one yelling, "What's for dinner, Ma?," the realization that you're not needed takes your breath away. It's painful! So you pick up the phone and call them, get all up in their business in an effort to make yourself indispensable. I had already lost two of my kids to college and had one on the verge of going; my ego couldn't take losing my last child—my business. By reinserting myself into the company, I was trying to pull my "adult child" back into the house with me. It wasn't good for my team, and it wasn't good for me.

The truth is, our kids still need us after they go off to college, and our team still needs us when they're running the business on their own. They just need us *in a different way*.

Dealing with your own bruised ego is just one of the ways you—and others in your organization—may resist the streamlining process I've detailed in this book. When you start implementing the Clockwork system, you may experience blowback or resistance from your team, partners, colleagues, friends, family . . . and yourself. Expect it. Plan for it. And above all, be patient with yourself and others. Change is hard, man. We're only human beings. And human beings are notorious for being awfully human.

IT FEELS CONTRARY TO WHAT WILL WORK

The greatest irony is that while building systems is hard work, it is not busywork. You won't be typing away all the time. You won't be meeting with people all the time. You won't be busy. You will be focusing on the hardest work of all—thinking.

Thinking about your business—*Designing* your business—takes a lot of energy and concentration. So, because we're humans, the natural instinct is to distract ourselves by doing the work. It may sound crazy that hard work is easier than hard thinking, but it is.

Just like if you had two options: 1) Try to dig a ditch in fifteen minutes, or 2) try to solve a Rubik's Cube in fifteen minutes. The ditch, even as hard as it is physically, for many people, will be easier to complete. Since we are almost guaranteed to see a result with the ditch, many people will turn to that. Or try the Rubik's Cube for just a few minutes and get frustrated that the @#$! yellow center square is still on the @#$! other side from all the other @#$! yellow pieces. So then we throw the cube down, and run outside into the rain and dig the ditch. Thinking takes a lot of energy, a lot of patience, and a lot of concentration.

Also, when we are "thinking" and "not doing," it feels as though we are not bringing benefit to our business, because we often don't get immediate results from thinking. We want the instant gratification of checking tasks off a list, filling a quota, delivering services, reaching a goal.

The truth is, the thinker is getting *serious* stuff done. They even dedicated a statue to him—you know, *The Thinker*—because he has figured out that the goal is not to do stuff, but instead to think about how to get the things done. Getting shit done is not the goal. The goal is to have the *company* get shit done. Instead of doing the work, you need to be *thinking* about the work, and who you can get to do it.

Don't fool yourself into believing that just because you're sitting there with your chin resting on your fist—naked—that you are not working. Heck, everyone knows the best ideas come when you're in the shower! Why? Because you are not doing work—no email, no calls, none of that. You are doing the most important work: thinking. I now seek out saunas whenever I'm traveling because they are like showers on steroids (I can't do anything in there . . . including moving). I just sit and think, and sure enough I get my best work done in them.

Want to know how to design a business that runs itself just like clockwork? Ask yourself big powerful questions and let your mind work on it. And remember, just because you're naked doesn't mean it's not work!

PUSHBACK FROM PARTNERS

I can't tell you how many times my business partner said, "You aren't doing enough for the business. We need more of you." I get why Ron felt this way. He was still caught up in the "do everything" mentality. Everything is important. Everything is critical. Everything is urgent. Ron would say, "You used to run circles around this place. I've never seen someone work so hard. Now you are never around." Which, you and I know, is because of the move from the Doing to the Designing phase, but to the outside world—or even your business partner—it may look as if you have just abandoned the business.

Ron has a heart of gold. I admire him, and I know how much he cares for our business, and for our clients, and for our mission of eradicating entrepreneurial poverty. He takes everything to heart, and he wants everyone to have an extraordinary experience. I trust him more than anyone in the business world.

When we started to streamline Profit First Professionals, we used one of our quarterly meetings to explain to all employees what I do to serve the QBR, and how they are supporting it. I explained that Profit First was a concept I had created eight years before the business even existed, including it in my first book and subsequently expanding on it in an article I wrote for the *Wall Street Journal.* It was the time I had to work on the concept and improve it that made it a reality. I explained that my job now was making strategic moves. Planning the big moves. Spreading the word, and finding others who can spread the word. When I started PFP, I had to do it all. It was just me and Ron, after all, and we were both needed for the Doing. Now I was needed as a Designer.

Ron and I met privately and I asked for more help getting the day-to-day off my plate, and he was not happy about it. We had a lot of tough, heated conversations in which he asserted that I had to spend more time working *in* the business and less time writing and speaking. As I said earlier, our QBR is spreading the message of eradicating entrepreneurial poverty, so what he was asking me for would not help us grow our business but would actually restrict it. But for Ron, who was busy all day, every day, my plan seemed counterintuitive.

His understandable pushback against my efforts to make PFP run without me (and him) came to a head when we hired a new employee, Billie Anne. She was quite capable with tech, which thrilled me, because up until that point, I was the only person in-house who had the skill set to work on technology. With more experience in this space than the other five full-timers at our office combined, I was the obvious choice to head up our app development work. But because I was focused on trying to serve the QBR, and because I still hadn't removed myself from managing other projects, I only got around to working on our tech project sporadically.

At the time, we were developing software that would be essential for PFP members. I had been leading the project for five months but had only managed to get the software to the point where it was functional but not usable. It wasn't yet at the level that would make our members want to work with it, indicated by the fact that even after the first release of the software they still preferred just working with spreadsheets and paper.

I met with Ron, gave him an update about the project, and said, "I want to give this to Billie Anne. She can handle it."

Ron was adamant that I stay the course. He said, "When you take something on, Mike, it's your responsibility to see it through. You've got to work harder. Push through."

What Ron was saying wasn't wrong; it was consistent with his experience, but that experience was not consistent with operational efficiency; instead, it was consistent with the brute force approach of "just be more productive." I blame it on lacrosse.

Growing up, Ron and I were on the same lacrosse team in high school. Ron was a better player than I was (and, I recently discovered, still is, when he schooled me in a face-off at a recent alumni game). Everyone on the team has to pull their weight, plus some. Ron knew the golden rule of lacrosse all too well: when any player is down or not playing well, the team captains have to play harder. You don't seek to do less, you toughen up and do more and more and more. Of course, a lacrosse game is a sprint. The entire playing time is one hour. Business is a marathon, the entire "game" being played over years, decades, or a lifetime.

"We're not the players on the lacrosse team, Ron," I told him. "We're the team owners. We have to act like owners, and since we haven't hired the coaches yet, you need to serve that role as I serve our QBR. We need to coach our team, our employees, and give them the strategy to win. We're off the field now."

I think he heard what I said, but it didn't land. That meeting didn't end well. So, out of respect for Ron, I stayed on as lead for the tech project. What I *did* do was run a test, with Ron's permission. I had Billie Anne help me with one tiny piece of the project, which she knocked out in no time. Then I went back to Ron, told him I got one piece done with Billie Anne's help, and showed him the results.

Ron said, "Wow! She's fast. Let's do that again," and he agreed to let Billie Anne take on more and more of the tasks. Now she's leading the project. Over the course of three weeks, I convinced him, by showing him Billie Anne's results, that it would be better if I pulled out of the project. More important, he convinced himself. Ron is smart and thirsts to learn, but just like you and me, he is comfortable with the familiar. He worked harder on the field than any other lacrosse player, me included. He worked harder at work than any of his colleagues, hence his success. But now he had to let go of the comfort of hard work and start supporting choreographed work. Sometimes your biggest resistance, if it doesn't come from you, will come from your business partners or executive team. They are human and need guidance with change. Take small steps toward organizational efficiency, and prove through tests that everyone on your executive team needs to move toward Designing and away from Doing.

Now, because I'm not working on the software project, I have time to meet with international partners and negotiate international contracts for PFP. Under the leadership of Femke Hogema, we opened a new location in the Netherlands and brought on thirty members with little effort. We then launched a location in Australia with Laura Elkaslassy, and she is already proving she can serve the community (and grow our organization) in extraordinary ways. Next up: Mexico, or Japan, or somewhere else. They are in the works, but the QBR is always the priority.

You will be challenged by partners who are still playing like team captains—not coaches or owners. It's not because they are wrong, or bad. It's because they are doing what they have always done. Work with your partners. Meet them halfway, and then halfway again, until they finally see the benefits of organizational efficiency.

I did a quick day trip to Chicago and met up with my longtime friend Rich Manders. His company, Freescale Coaching, has been so successful in bringing efficiency, growth, and profitability to companies that prospects are putting down $10,000 deposits to have the privilege of getting his coaching a year or more from now. Yes, he is that good.

We were walking down Michigan Avenue to a group meeting we were attending, and I asked Rich, "With all your success helping companies grow, what would you say is the most common and biggest roadblock businesses need to get past?" I fully expected something about the finances, marketing, and/or the product mix.

Rich looked at me and said, "That's easy. It's always a lack of communication and clarity among the executive team. Always."

Clockwork is not a system for you. It is a system for your entire company. Everyone needs to know it. Everyone needs to be on the same page. Everyone needs to begin moving the leadership from Doing to Designing.

PUSHBACK FROM EVERYONE ELSE

As you move into the Design role and shift your business to the optimal 4D Mix, you will likely get pushback from other people—your staff, your vendors, your shareholders (if you have them), and even your customers. Pushback from these groups is easier to deal with than the pushback from partners, because, ultimately, you're in charge; you're not sharing in the decisions with someone who has equal decision-making authority.

Pushback does not mean that you are on the wrong track, nor does it mean you have to barrel through conflicts that come up without a second thought. Expect to meet resistance along the way and plan for a strategy to address it in advance. This will help you manage it. Ultimately, pushback comes from a place of fear and insecurity. Clear communication goes a long way in mitigating some of those feelings, as does managing expectations, listening to questions and concerns, and providing reassurance.

Some people feel strongly about traditions, legacy, and company culture. Listening to their feedback will help you to make the transition to a Clockwork business smooth and successful. After all, you can't anticipate every mistake or wrong turn, but the people who do business with you now can certainly help you spot them.

When Ruth Soukup of Living Well Spending Less began working with Adrienne Dorison on clockworking her business, she identified the company's QBR as product design. They create products that help women simplify their lives, and their business growth depends on improving on those deliverables and creating new offerings.

Ruth is the primary person serving her company's QBR. She authored a *New York Times* bestselling book *Living Well, Spending Less* and creates planners and other helpful tools. It won't surprise you to learn that Ruth discovered she was wearing too many hats, and that she needed to let her staff take on some of her duties. She and Adrienne set a goal of freeing up three "coffee shop" days a week—time when Ruth could focus on design and expanding her vision for the company. It soon became clear that in order to meet this and other goals, she would have to add people to her team. Ruth brought on a new CMO (chief marketing officer) and a creative director, which helped immensely.

As Ruth told Adrienne, "Giving me three days of 'focus time' has forced every department to adjust to support that goal. They track how many times I meet that goal, which is one of their metrics. We're not there yet, but we're getting there. Everyone is working well together and stepping up to do what needs to get done."

Ruth went on to explain that, for the first time in the history of her company, she was not stressed out during a major product launch. Since she began applying Clockwork to her business, she also has had zero employee turnover.

Ruth also addressed the way her team handled conflict and put a system in place for acknowledging concerns and finding solutions. For example, up until then, Ruth had been the only person focused on revenue and cash flow. When she tasked her team with meeting specific revenue goals, she initially met some resistance. It wasn't that they didn't want to focus on revenue; it was just a new way of looking at their roles in the company.

"I can't even tell you how amazing it is," Ruth added. "When we started this process, our fourth quarter sucked. We had just added a lot of people and we had two poor-performing months. My team came to me and assured me we were doing the right thing, and to trust that we could handle it. They took the reins, created a new product in four days, and crushed it."

With the team supporting Ruth's goals and specific solutions and outcomes, the company had a record-earning next quarter. Ruth said, "The more I see their efforts, the more I am willing to trust my team. I am so grateful they fight for what they believe in, for margin, and for me, because they know that's important."

As your business begins to tick along beautifully, you will be met with resistance from the usual suspects—your staff and your partners—and from people you don't expect. Your family may question your new freedom and express concern about potential cash flow problems. Your colleagues may wonder why you turned in your workaholic badge and give you a hard time about your new way of running your business. No matter who pushes back against the way you now run your business, remember that they, just like you, are only human. They'll get there. And so will you. The proof's in the pudding, as they say: a profitable business that runs like clockwork.

CLOCKWORK IN ACTION

Start having active conversations about your vision and plan for your business. Talk with and listen to your partners, colleagues, vendors, clients, and family. Open, active dialogue greases many wheels in transitioning a business to run itself. Action is everything, so start the conversation now. Or, better yet, instead of interrupting the people around you, take the action of getting it on your calendar *and* theirs.

CHAPTER TEN

THE FOUR-WEEK VACATION

"Two years from now my family and I will be living in Italy. We will be sipping on limoncellos from our apartment balcony overlooking Rome."

When Greg Redington made that announcement to our mastermind group during our perfunctory pre-meeting personal updates, it caught everyone's attention. It wasn't what we expected to hear. When one of us asks, "Anything cool going on?" the replies typically are one of the famous three: "Nah, nothing new," "All is good," or "I've got this weird pain in my [fill in the blank]." But Italy? Huh? WTF?

At first, we thought Greg was joking, that he was just making a flippant comment. When we realized he was serious, we were all taken aback.

"Greg, do you mean Italy, Italy? Like the boot-shaped country? Or are you talking about that new Little Italy neighborhood popping up in your town?" I asked, still confused about the prospect of leaving his booming business in New Jersey to head to another country, permanently. Or at least permanently enough that he was going to declare Rome as his new hometown and the Pantheon as his favorite stop for a morning cup o' joe.

Greg is the founder of REDCOM Design & Construction LLC, a commercial construction management firm serving New York and New Jersey. He had grown his business into a substantial company, earning $25 million in annual revenue. He enjoyed the work tremendously, but the business was still dependent on him. Greg wanted more out of life and more time *in* his life. He wanted to be released from serving the QBR.

Greg's gift is meticulousness. You see it in the way he dresses, the home he keeps, even in the way he talks. He is specific. He is detailed. He is exacting. REDCOM has built its reputation on that meticulousness. In an industry where construction errors, redos, and on-the-fly changes are commonplace, REDCOM does the project right from start to finish. They build magnificent structures, perfectly . . . you know, like the Pantheon, but in New Jersey. But up until this point, Greg was serving the QBR. As the final step of designing his business to run itself, he had to step out of serving the QBR. And he wanted to do it in grand fashion, by living out a long-held dream.

When my fellow masterminders pushed Greg for more details, he explained that he had wanted to move his family to Rome, Italy, for a year. To do that, he committed to the final stage of establishing a Clockwork business. He removed himself from his business, to a point where it had to stand on its own. And the result was astonishing. Greg returned from Italy after two years, to a business that was now double its size, doing $50 million in annual revenue and with double the staff.

That's what I'm working toward, and what I call on you to work toward. Not the number, but the freedom where you can leave the business and have it still drive forward. You've already made significant headway in that direction. You've gone through the seven-step process, and hopefully, you've already started to see improvements in business efficiency. You've calmed your mind and developed systems. Heck, just by reading this book all the way through you're further along than most entrepreneurs. It is time to schedule your four-week vacation.

You can do this. I promise you, you can. And sure, maybe some people will think you're joking when you tell them your plan. You may get pushback from your friends, who may be jealous because, for whatever reason, they are not able to take a four-week vacation. You may get strong pushback from your family, who may be nervous about money. And you may—scratch that, you *surely* will—get pushback from your colleagues, who don't believe that taking a four-week vacation is possible or deserved for business owners. It's okay. In my experience, pushback from others is usually a sign that you're doing something that challenges the preprogrammed, drone-like mind-set that asserts things need to be the way they always were. Of course, you'll want to address your family's concerns about money so that they can enjoy the vacation (*cough*, read *Profit First*, *cough cough*), but ignore the rest. You've worked the system, and now you're going to reap the rewards.

Even if all you do with your four weeks off is sit in your backyard and watch the squirrels, you and your business will be better for it. After all, if your business can hold its own—and even experience growth—with you out of the picture, how much easier will it be to run your business when you get back? (Answer: Heaps. Tons. Loads easier.)

You don't need to leave that vacation behind, either. Greg didn't. After two years of living in Rome, it was tough for Greg to leave Italy. So when he returned to his company, he made sure he brought a little bit of Italy back with him. No, not a limoncello.

Greg brought back a Fiat Cinquecento. The fabled mini-car is parked inside his office's "hangar" for display and quick drives. On a warm spring day, Greg will take it for a little drive. Not all over town, of course, just in Little Italy.

And what about working in his business? Was Greg happy to return to serving the QBR? Actually, yes. That is the power of Clockwork. You aren't forced to leave your business; you are *freed* to leave. This means you are freed to do what your heart sings out to do. Greg thrives on leading detailed construction projects. When he returned from his dream of living in Italy, he did only the work he wanted to do. Greg has become a specialty player for his company. He no longer swoops in to "fix things." The company is running well on its own, and he is free to do the work he does best, and loves best. And the results are even more magnificent.

WHY A FOUR-WEEK VACATION?

Most businesses go through a full business cycle within four weeks. This means that most businesses have activity within all four of the ACDC stages of a business: Attract, Convert, Deliver, Collect. If you look at your business over the last month, it is likely there was some effort made to attract clients. Perhaps you had another client give you a referral, or you ran an ad, or you spoke at a conference, or you sent out an email blast, or you had visitors at your website, or a combination of all the above. It is also likely that during the past four weeks your business made an effort to convert prospects into new clients. Maybe you had a sales call, or your website has an active "buy now" option, or an automated email campaign asked for the sale. In short you tried (and hopefully have been able) to convince someone to buy from you.

During the last four weeks, you probably worked on a project for a client, or created a product, or shipped goods; you tried to deliver something in part or in whole per a request of a client. And throughout the last four weeks, you managed the cash flow; you probably paid some money out and (hopefully) brought some more in.

In a four-week cycle, most businesses will also experience internal issues or challenges, big or small—an interpersonal conflict on your team, a flu epidemic, a technology breakdown, someone will forget to do something, or someone will remember to do something but, unfortunately, it's the wrong thing. And during those four weeks you'll also probably deal with external problems, such as disgruntled customers or a competitor's new product launch or a banking error or a vendor failing to deliver on a promise.

When you are removed from the business for four weeks, it is likely that the vast majority of things your business faces on a daily basis will happen, so you must find a way for the work to get done and the problems to be solved in your absence. When you are gone only a few days, the business can often delay the resolution of problems until you return. But if you are gone for a few weeks, the business is forced to support itself. And when a business can support itself for four weeks, you know you have achieved a Clockwork business. You can put the certified stamp of Clockwork approval on your company's door, and now have the freedom to get out of Dodge permanently, if you like.

So let's put this mofo business to a test, and get you out of the office and to a destination elsewhere. Maybe it's Rome to sip on limoncellos with Greg and his wife. Or maybe you'd rather spend a month with a friend. No matter what you do with your time off, or where you go, we need to get you out of the office both physically and virtually. We need you out, without access to your team.

GO ON VACATION—FOR REAL

For years I pondered how to get out of my own businesses. No matter if I was doing the work, deciding for others about the work, delegating the work, or designing the work, I always felt trapped by the business. I was sure that I "just had to be there." As I shared in chapter one, even on the few occasions that I took a vacation, I really didn't "vacate"—I may have physically gone away, but I stayed connected. I would connect with the office multiple times during the day. I would check email constantly. I would "sneak away" to make client calls, to write proposals, to just work. Then one day I accidentally found how to take a *real* vacation, one that disconnects you from your business so that it needs to live on its own.

I went to Maine.

Now, there are plenty of places to visit in Maine that will allow you to stay connected to your business. The place we chose to visit—not so much. I booked a vacation at an all-inclusive camp in the Lakes and Mountains region of Maine, called Grant's Kennebago Camps. I fit the planning for the vacation into my busy work schedule, so in my haste I didn't fully evaluate the camp's website. I saw the "all-inclusive meals" part. I saw the beautiful lake. I saw pictures of families boating and having fun, all with big smiles on their faces.

What escaped my attention was that, in those pictures, mom and dad and their kiddos were wearing camouflage.

When we arrived at the camp, we quickly realized I had booked our family vacation at a hunting and fishing camp. And the only "family" part about the camp was that the campers were hunting families of *deer*.

We were totally disconnected from the outside world—no cell, no TV, no nothing. The only radio station we could find was broadcasting out of Canada . . . in French. I took Spanish in high school. *Yo no hablo francés-o.*

The first day I was in detox from constant connection. *Will the business die without me?* The second day, I began to analyze my options. *I could drive into town every day to check in.* The nearest town was an hour away, and I was seriously contemplating a two-hour round-trip commute to check in with work. *Or I could just enjoy the time with my family. All of it.* By the third day, I was at peace and loved the vacation.

I'm sure you're not surprised—the business didn't die. Did my team have problems? Sure. Did they fix the problems on their own? Some of them, yes. For those problems they couldn't solve, they bought time so I could fix them when I returned. They did a great job of managing our customers' expectations, which meant that, even though they did have problems, the customers knew their problems were being addressed.

We ended up having the time of our lives. We skipped rocks, hiked, and boated around the lake. We spotted geese and mooses! Or is it meese and gooses? The vacation was so powerful, right then and there we declared our family mascot as the moose. It is powerful and serene, even though the impression at first glance is that it is a little bit goofy, which is very much our family creed.

Today, I reflect back on that life-defining vacation and remember everything with such joy. Including the hysterical "bat attack" and "leech assault" stories that Krista and I will gladly share with you over dinner. We recall every single detail of those stories and more. The work I missed? I don't recall anything about it. In fact, I can't remember a single business initiative I had going on then.

As I write this book, I'm planning my four-week vacation, and at the top of my mind is how to ensure a disconnect. I need to guard against my own weakness to find excuses to "check in" and ruin the test. When you think about where you want to go on your vacation, and what you want to experience, take into account how connected you want to be. Remember my story about the first time I visited Australia? I was in a different, upside-down time zone than my team, and so I felt completely disconnected— even though I had email and could video call and text. And boy, did I use that technology to screw things up and annoy my team. Will you need to force the disconnect by choosing a place with limited options for you to check in with work? Maybe. It certainly helps. Remember, you are not taking this vacation as a necessary break from your business, as much as your business is getting a necessary break from you.

Design your vacation around the type of experience you and your loved ones would like to have, with the intent of being disconnected. The combination of enjoying yourself while away will help keep your mind off of the business, and the inability to connect will protect you from caving in to the temptation to "check in" and F everything up.

The goal behind planning your four-week vacation is to free you from your business so that the business can learn to run itself. This is the final step of the surgical operation of separating you from your conjoined twin, the business. And this is a test to make sure both you and your business can live without each other. If this exercise were a medicine bottle, the warning label would read "You may reclaim your life."

You need to do these steps now, even if you are a single-practitioner business, because even a single-practitioner business can find ways to have at least partial independence from the owner doing all the Doing. You can automate processes and deliverables. The technology exists and the subcontractors are out there to bring large amounts of independence to any size business.

The four-week vacation is designed for the owner of the business. You are the one we need to set free. And if you want to get your business to the highest Clockwork level (where it is pure smooth sailing), you can do a four-week vacation for your staff, too. My assistant, Kelsey, is going on a three-month sabbatical the same year that I am doing a four-week vacation, and we have already projected our best performing year yet.

The four-week vacation does not need to be something of extravagance. You can do it anywhere you want, and do it within a budget that you can afford. You just need to achieve certain goals:

1. Physically disconnect from the office.
2. Virtually disconnect from the office. There is a way to do this, even if there is cell and Wi-Fi where you are.
3. Let the business run for the entire time without you connecting. You can go to Maine (awesome) or you can go to your mother-in-law's (let's just say, that may not rank up there with Maine). But there is a budget-friendly way to do this. Your business needs you to do this so it can grow. *You* need to do this so *you* can grow.

OPERATION VACATION

When planning your four-week vacation, start by picking a date that is eighteen to twenty-four months from today. Yes, you can do it faster and split in six months. Or super fast and just split tomorrow. But that won't likely give you the time to prepare. If you plan your four-week vacation more than a year out, you'll have a chance to live and work through that same four weeks on the calendar year, which is crucial to effective planning.

Once you commit to your vacation, you will likely notice an immediate shift in your mind. First you'll have the "Oh, shit, what have I done" moment. That's normal. You'll get over that within twenty-four hours. Then you will notice your focus will no longer be on the super short term, or simply what is urgent now. Thoughts such as "How do I get through today?" will shift to "How can I make this happen without me?" "What needs to change so that this aspect of my business can run without dependency on me?"

To make your life easier, I have broken down the tasks you need to complete at various milestones. This will help you stay the course so you can actually *get* to Rome, or Maine, or Rome, Maine (yes, it exists), or wherever you want to hang for twenty-eight days.

EIGHTEEN MONTHS OUT—
DECLARE IT

1. Put your vacation dates on the calendar. Block it off. Do this *now*, as you read this. Don't delay. Your freedom and your company's success depend on it.
2. Tell your family, your loved ones, the people who will hold you accountable about your vacation—especially if they are coming with you! They will hold your feet to the fire.
3. Then declare it to me. If you haven't done so already, email me at Mike@OperationVacation.me, telling me that you are committing to the four-week vacation. To make sure I see it, please put in the subject line "My Clockwork commitment."

SIXTEEN MONTHS OUT—
RUN A TIME ANALYSIS

1. Run a Time Analysis of your work. At a minimum, complete all other Clockwork exercises for yourself.

FOURTEEN MONTHS OUT—
TELL YOUR TEAM

1. Tell your team about your commitment to your four-week vacation. Explain why you are doing this and the outcome you are hoping to achieve. Explain the benefit to the business, and to them.
2. Invite them to ask questions and share concerns. Empower them to achieve the outcome (remember the Delegating phase of business growth?).
3. Ask them for support in making this happen. Make it clear to them that you are not expecting them to work harder, or delay/defer people from speaking with you while you're away. Tell them the goal is to automate the business as much as possible. And the goal is never to defer or delay, because that does not address problems. The goal is for the problems to be addressed and/or fixed without you.
   a. If I may suggest, get them each a copy of *Clockwork* to read. That way they will know this process inside and out.
4. Establish better cross communication among team members.

    a. Have a clear line of responsibility for each role in the business (who is the person responsible that the job is done and done right), and have a backup person for each role if the primary person fails.

    b. Get a daily huddle going. You can do this in person or virtually, but it is a must. Review key performance metrics for the company. Have each person share the big thing they accomplished the day before, then share the big thing they are doing today and why it is important. Then give shout-outs to other employees, and share a personal update. A recording of one of my company's daily huddles is available at Clockwork.life.

TWELVE MONTHS OUT—
START TO CUT DOWN ON DOING

1. Have a meeting with your team to determine what you need to do to not be Doing. Write up an action plan to trash, transfer, and trim all your actions, including your QBR work.
2. Now that they've had two months to read up on the Clockwork system, have a discussion.
3. If you haven't already, have your team go through all the Clockwork exercises.
4. Within the next two months, commit to cutting down your Doing workload to be under 80 percent of your time. Trash, transfer, and trim. You may already be below 80 percent, and that is great. If that's the case, try to cut

another 10 percent of Doing work off your plate and push your time toward Designing.

5. Commit to putting in substitutes for the QBR so that you are not the only one serving it.

6. Visualize your four-week vacation and how it will affect your business. What do you anticipate will come up while you're away? How smoothly will your business run without you?

7. If you haven't done so already, book your vacation: make reservations, make deposits, buy tickets—whatever you need to do to make a full commitment. There's no turning back now, pal!

8. You can get professional help with organizational efficiency, too. Just as some people join a gym and work out of their own volition, others have much greater success when they get the guidance (and accountability) of a trainer. You can go to RunLikeClockwork.com to get a "trainer" to guide your business to run like, you know, clockwork.

TEN MONTHS OUT—
DEEPER CUTS TO DOING

1. Run a fresh Time Analysis on yourself. Confirm you are under 80 percent Doing or better.

2. Meet with your team to cut your Doing time to less than 40 percent. Allocate your freed-up time to Designing as much as possible.

EIGHT MONTHS OUT—
MEASURE PROGRESS AND ESTABLISH BACKUPS

1. Run a Time Analysis on yourself, again. Confirm you are at less than 40 percent Doing.
2. Commit to achieving 0 percent Doing time within the next sixty days.
3. Meet with your team to plan and measure progress.
4. Identify backups and redundancy for each person.

SIX MONTHS OUT—
RUN A TEST

1. Run a one-week vacation test. Head out of town to a place with no internet connection. Or do a virtual disconnect and stay home. Just don't go to the office and don't connect remotely.
2. Have a team meeting your first day back. Review what worked and what didn't. Make improvements and fixes.
3. Confirm plans for your four-week vacation.
4. Commit to reducing your Deciding and Delegating to 5 percent and Designing to 95 percent by two months out.

FOUR MONTHS OUT—
RUN MORE TESTS

1. Week 1, run another one-week vacation test. No connection for seven days.
2. Week 2, come back for a week. Meet with your team to debrief and fix the roadblocks to your four-week vacation.

3. Week 3, run another one-week vacation. No connection.
4. Week 4, meet again to debrief and fix.

TWO MONTHS OUT—
PLAN FULL DISCONNECT

1. Run another Time Analysis on yourself. Confirm you are at 0 percent Doing. If not, establish a plan to get there immediately.
2. Plan full disconnect with your team. Who will be responsible for monitoring your email, social media outlets, and other communication platforms? When you leave, they'll have to change your passwords and not give them to you until you return. That way they can manage it and you can't access it. Two birds. One stone.
3. Who will take your cell phone? If you will be near a landline, give that number to your team. Or you can get a four-week prepaid cell for emergencies.
4. Who will have your itinerary so that if a true emergency happens, they know where you are and how to contact you? This is in case of dying—personal or business.
5. Commit to 99 percent Design time. There is no such thing as 100 percent Design since, ultimately, you will have to share and roll out insights to your team, therefore Delegating work and Deciding for others. But the goal is for that time to be minimal.

ONE MONTH OUT—
ACT AS AN OBSERVER

1. Act as an observer of your business. Be tough on yourself. Make sure you are not Doing or Deciding.
2. Delegate the outcomes for any remaining work.
3. Allow Design time to naturally happen on your four-weeker. The goal of the four weeks is to test your business and ensure it can be free of you. You're an entrepreneur, which means even though you're disconnecting from day-to-day business operations, Design time will happen on this trip. We can't help ourselves! To prepare, accumulate the few tools that help Design time be productive when it happens. Visit your favorite office supplies store, or go online, and buy a small notepad that can fit in your pocket and (mini or contractible) pen to go with it. When you feel inspired, you can use these tools to capture your thoughts.
4. Look for any loose ends that you need to tie up. Don't tie them up; instead, document that you have loose ends. That is a problem, because a loose end is something that wasn't trashed, transferred, or trimmed. Give those loose ends to someone else.
5. Get anyone who is going on the four-weeker with you pumped. It is only four weeks until your four weeks!

ONE WEEK OUT—
TAKE A VACATION AT WORK

1. Take a vacation, so to speak, at the office. The goal here is to have no Doing work at all. You shouldn't have a

deadline for anything, except for self-imposed stuff. This is where you have moved to focus on what is important, and not what is urgent. In fact, you shouldn't even be aware of what is urgent at this point. Your team should be handling all but the most serious emergency.

2. If you have anything besides Design work that consumes your time, Delegate it to your team. This includes any task you've secretly been hoarding for yourself. You know, the thing that, even after all this streamlining, you still think only you can do. Yes, I'm looking at you. I know you. I know you like I know my twin (if I had one). We're cut from the same cloth, my friend. Time to let go of that one last thing . . .

THE DAY BEFORE OPERATION VACATION

1. Send your last email (for the next four weeks, that is) to me at Mike@OperationVacation.me with the subject line "I'm outta here!" I am your accountability partner and need to know that you have pulled off your commitment before you head out.

2. Have your assistant—or whomever you delegated to check your accounts—change your email, Facebook, and any other passwords so that only they can see them.

3. Get your ass in the car. You have a vacation to get to!

WHILE YOU ARE AWAY

1. I am not good at meditating in the traditional sense. Sitting criss-cross applesauce while saying *om* is just uncom-

fortable in so many ways for me. But I do find that I get lost in moments, or daydream. I don't know when these things will happen, but I do know when they don't happen . . . when I am focused on work. But if I just chill, hike, bike, sit in a coffee shop, sit in a sauna, take a long shower, those magic moments of pure genius happen. *Let it happen.*

2. Have a notepad at the ready. Always. I have a little spiral book that fits in my pocket with a pen. And my phone has a voice recorder that I use to record thoughts and ideas. Just because you're off work for four weeks doesn't mean you can't record business insights or goals that you can review when you get back.

3. Make meaningful connections. One of the first things to shift down the priority list when we're on the grind is time with our loved ones, friends, and even total strangers who may have something to share with us. We move too fast for meaningful connections. Now that you're away, make a point to listen to those you love, to stop and talk to a fellow tourist, vendor, or busker on the street.

4. Take pictures. You'll probably do this anyway, but the reason I'm adding this obvious task to your list is because you need at least one memorable picture that exemplifies your four-week vacation experience. Why? Because when you get back, you're going to frame it and hang it in your office as a visual reminder of all that you accomplished—and as inspiration for your next trip.

WHEN YOU RETURN

1. Have a debrief meeting scheduled for the day after you return to the office. And schedule one a week for the next four weeks. We are going to debrief, improve, review, improve, review, improve.
2. In your meetings, evaluate what worked and what didn't. What went as you expected? What surprise challenges came up? What did you forget to handle before you left? What areas need improvements? The four-week vacation will magnify what you didn't plan for or expect. Set out to fix and improve those things.
3. Schedule your next four-week vacation for twelve months from now. This will be a regular thing. And then perhaps you want to go for the big one: the fifty-two-week vacation. Or maybe the ultimate: the forever vacation.

You will notice that nowhere throughout this process did I say, "Notify your clients that you will be away for four weeks." The ultimate success is when your customers say, "I didn't realize you were away." Of course, if you are in a business in which your absence would put your customers at risk, you should tell them. For example, if you are a doctor, you may have a patient reach out with an emergency. Or if you have fifty accounting clients and will be away during the last four weeks of tax season (that would be badass if you committed to that), you may want to give them notice and explain how you are addressing it. I prefer not to notify clients, but use your professional discretion.

I get it. I'm asking you to do something that at this time in your life may seem impossible. How are you going to plan for a four-week vacation when you're operating on four *hours* of sleep every day? I want to inspire you to make this commitment, of course, but I know from experience that it's more important that you make a smaller commitment.

Over the years, I've heard from countless entrepreneurs and business owners who follow Profit First—almost. Many people don't follow the whole system. They do the minimum required— they set aside a small percentage for profit with each deposit. Even this one tiny change has had a dramatic effect on their businesses. So much so that many people whisper their successes to me, as if they can't believe that simply setting aside profit first could work such magic on their business's growth and bottom line.

So now, even though I want you to plan for this vacation so that you can design your business to run itself, I am asking you to lower the bar. Keep it simple. Start by committing to two changes for your business:

1. Take 1 percent Design time.
2. Declare your QBR.

A small amount of Design time can help you implement the other steps in this book, or can help you come up with your next great product idea or a solution to a problem. Similarly, simply being *aware* of your QBR will change the way you operate on a day-to-day basis.

Two changes. That's it. You can do it. When you get good at these two things, you can take on more. This book will be here when you're ready to go "full Clockwork." And I'll be here for you, no matter what.

CLOSING

met Ryan Lee about an hour before I was to arrive at MSNBC's studios to film a segment for their entrepreneurial show, *Your Business*, hosted by JJ Ramberg. Occasionally, I am allowed to bring a guest to check out the show, and while the booker was confirming my arrival time that morning she mentioned that I was welcome to bring one to this taping.

Even with a fun tour of the MSNBC studios and the *Saturday Night Live* studios at the fabled 30 Rock building in New York City on offer, it is hard to find people with enough flexibility in their schedule to tag along, even when you give them notice weeks or months in advance.

I had known of Ryan for years but had not yet met him in person. As a shot in the dark, I invited him to join me at the studio an hour before taping. He texted me back a few seconds later. "I would love to. I was going to head to the movies, but that can easily wait. See you in an hour."

The movies? This was a Thursday midmorning taping. Surely, Ryan had taken the day off in advance to take one of his children to the movies for their birthday. Or maybe he was decompressing for a couple of hours, from an insanely demanding schedule.

When I met Ryan face-to-face, I found my assumptions couldn't have been further from the truth. The reality was, Ryan runs Freedym, a multimillion-dollar business with just a couple of virtual employees and works only a few hours a week. The rest of the time he spends thinking about his business. Strategizing about his business. Monitoring his business. He enjoys his hobby of watching movies, and his favorite activity is spending time with his wife and kids. He's with them nearly every day of the year.

So there I sat, in the green room as the makeup specialist troweled foundation onto my face in preparation for my segment, and drilled Ryan with questions.

"You are the first person that I've ever met that has such flexibility in their schedule, and also has a booming business. What am I missing here?"

Ryan picked up a grape and threw it in the air to catch in his mouth; it bounced off his cheek. He started answering my question as he made his next grape-catching attempt, which was successful.

"You need a system, Mike. You need a system that you know at the start of every day you are going to follow throughout the entire day. And then only react when something unexpected happens. Otherwise you monitor its progress, and if you are not satisfied with its performance, you make small tweaks and adjustments."

He picked up a grape, motioning to me to do an open-mouth catch, and threw it across the room. I quickly leaned to the side to catch it, and the makeup artist, not expecting my sudden movement, ran blush (meant to make my cheeks a little rosier) up my nose, which made my nose very rosy. In one fell swoop, I looked like I enjoyed the hooch a little *too* much. The grape flew past, bounced off the trowel, and landed harmlessly on the floor.

Ryan continued without missing a beat. "We never really had a specific, repeatable process for getting new customers. We tried a little social media here, and a few ads there. But it was sporadic. I couldn't really measure if something worked. I had no understanding of what was 'normal' for us and therefore no way to know what I needed to improve.

"But then we created a system that we had managed by one person," he continued. "We repeated it daily. Measured it. And slowly but surely improved it, but never deviated from it. Now we knew exactly what we were doing every day to get customers. We knew the one place to put our ads. We knew what copy to write, what headline to use, and what images to use. Then we would simply measure it. If my metrics showed that it wasn't working well, we tweaked it—one element at a time—until it did work."

Another grape launched in the air. And Ryan caught it dead center in his mouth; I heard the snapping sound as the grape hit his tongue.

"Our revenue doubled. We have predictability. And I have delegated the process to a colleague who runs it and makes decisions on getting it right. I just watch the numbers, and if something doesn't look right, I investigate. And now I spend a lot of time doing my favorite things in the world: being with my family and watching *Teen Wolf*, the best movie ever, for the hundredth time."

Everything Ryan told me was spot on. Everything he said works. Everything he said was right, except for *Teen Wolf* being the best movie ever. We all know it is *Terminator 2*.

Ryan's story is not special. It's not lightning in a bottle, something only a few people get to experience. It's also not about luck, or karma, or how hard he worked when he started his company. It's not about the dues he paid or the people he knows. It's all down to the systems. Your business may be limping along or stuck in a rut. Maybe it's drowning in work, or debt, or both. You may be just starting out or ready to give up. Whatever your circumstances, you can have your own version of Ryan's story.

Ryan isn't smarter than you or luckier than you. In fact, he used to tough it out in his business, too. He worked like an animal, dealt with crushing business debt, didn't take a paycheck for three years so he could ensure his employees would be paid. As a result of the stress, Ryan eventually developed pain in his hands so severe he couldn't open a jar. His feet hurt so much he could barely walk. Today, he's in good health, and so is his business.

No matter what you have or don't have; no matter what challenges you face and what mistakes you've made; no matter *what*, you can grow a profitable business that runs itself. Before you cracked this book, you may not have known how to do that. Now you're armed with a system that's doable.

I believe this system works. And I believe in you. Actually, I know this system works, and I'm certain you can pull it off.

I can't wait to see your vacation pictures from Maine. Or Spain. Or Antarctica. Or wherever you plan to go for your four-week vacation.

Let's get busy designing your business to run itself . . . like clockwork.

ACKNOWLEDGMENTS

I think, in some strange way, being an author of a book is like being the front man of a band. The front man gets all the attention, and not just because he is wearing awkwardly tight spandex trousers, but because he's the one standing at the front of the stage screaming into a microphone. Yet there wouldn't be any music without the entirety of the band. It takes everyone working in harmony to make beautiful music. It's a bit unfair that the front man gets all the attention. Just like it is unfair that I, being the author, get all the attention. There is a powerful band alongside me up on stage. Let me introduce them to you:

On drums is Anjanette "AJ" Harper. If I am the soul of my books, she is the heart. Every one of my books has been a collaborative writing effort between myself and AJ. She is a relentless stickler for quality in writing and clarity in communication. By far, *Clockwork* has been the most challenging project we have done together. After six years of work and even throwing out an entire manuscript (seriously), the project is complete. *Clockwork* is the best of me and it is the best of Anjanette. Thank you, AJ.

Our song composer is Kaushik Viswanath. Kaushik (pronounced "the world's best editor") never accepts good enough. Never. He tore *Clockwork* down to the studs and helped rebuild it into a far better book. *Clockwork* is exponentially better because of Kaushik's effort and commitment to quality. Thank you, Kaushik.

On lead guitar is Liz Dobrinska. I have worked with Liz for over ten years. Every website, every graphic, and even the cover of *Clockwork* has been created by Liz. Her ability to take my ideas and bring them to life blows me away every time. Thank you, Liz.

On rhythm guitar is Amber Dugger. I call her my Glam BLaM: my Glamorous Book Launch Manager. She is the one who got the word out on *Clockwork* before the manuscript was even done and continues to tirelessly grow the awareness. Everything she does, she does from the heart (that's the Glam part of Glam BLaM). She is spreading the word on *Clockwork* because it is the right thing to do. Thank you, Amber.

On bass is Adrienne Dorison. The bass is that one instrument that ties all the other sounds together. Adrienne is doing that with *Clockwork*. She launched RunLikeClockwork.com specifically to deliver *Clockwork* support to the entrepreneurs who need it. She is the only person I trust with such an important responsibility. (Plus, she really, really knows her shit.) Thank you, Adrienne.

On backup vocals is Kelsey Ayres. I will never be able to express my full gratitude to be working with Kelsey. She is more than my personal assistant. She is my right hand, my full brain, and a remarkable friend. And she just happens to be the kindest soul to have ever walked this planet. I am humbled to work with you, Kelsey. I am forever grateful for your tireless efforts in serving entrepreneurs with *Clockwork*. Thank you, Kelsey.

Last but not least is my greatest fan (she's kind of a groupie)— my wife, Krista. From the bottom of my heart I thank you and our children for supporting my dream of writing books that will eradicate entrepreneurial poverty. I love you and the kids more than I can ever express. Thank you for our journey together. I live you (that's not a typo).

GLOSSARY OF KEY TERMS

ACDC. The four major stages in the flow of business are: Attracting prospects, Converting prospects into clients, Delivering the promised offering to clients, and Collecting payment in return. Most businesses flow in the ACDC sequence, but it is not necessary. Some businesses, for example, collect payment before delivering services. And others may deliver a service before the prospect becomes a client.

Active Time Analysis. This is the process of tracking how you, or someone you work with, typically spends their time at work. Use this tool to discover how much time you devote to each of the 4Ds.

Cheetos. Just disgusting. Unless you are throwing back some beers. Then they aren't too shabby. Throw back even more beer, and then Cheetos, almost magically, become pretty damn tasty.

The Commitment. Once you determine your business's ideal offering (based on your ability and desires), you identify the type of customer it will best serve and commit to concentrating your efforts on serving that customer type.

Fat Daddy Fat Back. The name of my rapper alter ego. Do I really have a second career as a rapper? Maybe you should Google it and find out.

The Four Ds (4Ds). The four types of activities, and four phases of work, that any individual in a company will spend their time engaged in. They will either be Doing the work, Deciding about the work for others, Delegating the work to others, or Designing how the work gets done. In many cases, individuals will be doing a combination of the 4Ds.

Four-Week Vacation. Most businesses experience all of their activities within a four-week period. Therefore, if you, as a leader of the business, remove yourself from the company for a four-week consecutive period, your business will be forced to run itself. By making a commitment to a four-week vacation, you will immediately be in the mind-set of setting up your company to run itself.

Grant's Kennebago Camps. It is a bit of a tradition for our family now. None of us hunt or fish, so we are always the oddballs. But now it is part of us. Should you ever go and we run into you, please ask my wife to share the "bat story" . . . it is a family fave.

Miss Maud Hotel. A must-visit institution in Perth, Australia. Go for the smorgasbord and try the apple turnovers. They're to die for.

Operation Vacation. A movement of *Clockwork* readers (and others) who are allocating time for themselves first and building their business around it. Similar to the Profit First method of first allocating profit, then reverse-engineering the business to ensure that profit happens.

The Optimal 4D Mix. The optimal mix for a company is 80 percent Doing, 2 percent Deciding, 8 percent Delegating, and 10 percent Designing. This is not the optimal mix for the entrepreneur or business owner, and not necessarily the optimal mix for employees; it is the optimal mix for the entire business (which is made up of the work contribution of many individuals).

Parkinson's Law. The theory that people expand their consumption of a resource to meet its supply. For example, the more time that is allocated for a project, the longer it will take to complete.

Primary Job. This is the most critical role that an employee serves in their job. It needs to be prioritized over any other work.

Profit First method. This is the process of allocating a predetermined percentage of your company's income directly to a profit account before anything else is done with the money. The profit allocation occurs before paying bills. The entire process is documented in my book *Profit First.*

QBR. The Queen Bee Role. This is the one core function of your business that your success hinges on.

Solopreneur. A person who exclusively owns and operates their business.

Survival Trap. The Survival Trap is the never-ending cycle of reacting to the urgent at the cost of disregarding the important. This makes business survival a day-to-day emergency. Building a Clockwork business gets you out of the Survival Trap.

Top Client. The best client(s) of your business, as determined by you. Typically this is the client that pays you the most and whom you enjoy working with. The process of identifying and cloning your Top Client is documented in my book *The Pumpkin Plan.*

Trash, Transfer, and Trim. Take one of these three steps to remove work that distracts an individual from serving the QBR or their Primary Job. This process typically moves Doing and Deciding work to "lower level" employees and elevates Designing and Delegating to "higher level" employees.

AUTHOR'S NOTE

Thank you for reading *Clockwork*. It is my deepest desire to help you achieve the business you envision. I hope *Clockwork* has taken you one significant step closer to just that.

I would like to ask a small favor of you. No obligation whatsoever.

Would you be willing to post an honest review of *Clockwork*?

I ask because reviews are the most effective way for fellow entrepreneurs and business leaders to discover the book and determine if it will be of value to them. A review from you, even a single sentence or two, will achieve just that. To do it, simply go to the website (or the website for the store) where you bought the book and submit the review.

Again, I seek only your honest feedback. If you loved *Clockwork*, please say so. If you loathed the book, please share that, too (just try to refrain from calling me bad names). And if you are indifferent about the book, share that, too.

What matters the most is that other entrepreneurs hear your truth about *Clockwork*.

Thank you. I am wishing you your most successful year yet. You rock!

Mike

INDEX

Also by Mike Michalowicz

MikeMichalowicz.com

PORTFOLIO
PENGUIN

Want Mike to keynote your next event?

CONNECT WITH MIKE

Li Hayes ▪ Speaking Coordinator for Mike Michalowicz
888-244-2843 x7008 ▪ Li@MikeMichalowicz.com
MikeMichalowicz.com/Speaking